Sundays at the Magic Monastery

Sundays at the Magic Monastery

*Homilies from the Trappists
of St. Benedict's Monastery*

Thomas Keating • Theophane Boyd
William Meninger • Joseph Boyle

Lantern Books • New York
A Division of Booklight Inc.

2002
Lantern Books
One Union Square West, Suite 201
New York, NY 10003

© St. Benedict's Monastery, Snowmass, CO 2002

Scripture texts taken from the New American Bible, © Confraternity of Christian Doctrine, Washington, D.C., 1970, 1998.

Printed in the United States of America

Library of Congress Cataloging-in-Publication Data

Sundays at the magic monastery : homilies from the Trappists of St. Benedict's Monastery / Theophane Boyd ... [et al.].
     p. cm.
  ISBN 1-59056-033-7 (alk. paper)
  1. Church year sermons. 2. Catholic Church—Sermons. 3. Sermons, American—20th century. 4. Bible. N.T. Gospels—Sermons. I. Boyd, Theophane.
  BX1756.A2 S885 2002
  252'.02—dc21

                                                    2002006013

The homilies contained in this book, except for Chapter 16, "The Publican, the Pharisee, and Me" by William Meninger, which was delivered later, were originally recorded on audiocassette during the years 1996 and 1997 at St. Benedict's Monastery in Snowmass, Colorado—known affectionately as the Magic Monastery. The homilies are organized in the order of the Church year, beginning and ending at Advent. The homilies have been edited and rewritten for publication, but every effort has been made to capture the immediacy and spirit of the homilies that make Sundays at the Magic Monastery such a captivating and challenging experience.

Theophane Boyd is the author of *Tales of the Magic Monastery*. **Joseph Boyle** is the abbot at St. Benedict's Monastery. **Thomas Keating** is the bestselling author of several books, including *Open Mind, Open Heart* and *Fruits and Gifts of the Spirit*. **William Meninger** is the author of *The Process of Forgiveness* and *The Loving Search for God*. All four live at St. Benedict's Monastery.

—The Editors, Lantern Books

Table of Contents

1

Let Him In!

THEOPHANE BOYD

The First Sunday of Advent

Jesus said to his disciples, "Be on your guard. Stay awake, because you never know when the time will come. It's like a man traveling abroad. He's gone from home and left his servants in charge, each with his own task. And he's told the doorkeeper to stay awake. So, stay awake, because you do not know when the Master of the house is coming—evening, midnight, cock crow, dawn. If he comes unexpectedly he must not find you asleep. And what I say to you, I say to all. Stay awake!" (Mark 13:33-37)

This passage has a special importance because in St. Mark's Gospel these are Our Lord's final words before he goes to his death. They are very different from the final words in St. John's Gospel, and the passage is what is often called apocalyptic discourse. Some scholars call it persecution literature. In other words, this section offers the kind of writing that would arise if you were being persecuted, and the Jews felt themselves to be persecuted because they were dominated by the Romans.

Here, just before he goes to his death, Our Lord is addressing not the crowd, but four of his disciples—Peter, James, John, and Andrew. He uses this kind of persecution talk, which had to be symbolic, because if you got literal about what the Romans were doing, you were going to add to your troubles. Not only is the talk symbolic, but it takes on cosmic dimensions. This persecution was terrible; Jesus was going to be handed over, betrayed, beaten up, mocked, and put to death. So the persecution literature expresses this ordeal through the metaphor of the cosmos. The sun is darkened, the stars are falling down from the sky, earthquakes, famines, war—nothing too literal and pointed that the Romans or anybody else could get irritated about. But people hearing it knew what Our Lord was talking about.

This text was written possibly forty years after Our Lord's death—and St. John's discourse was written even later than that. It is not a verbatim report at all—it can't be, forty years later; but the author of this gospel, and the people he was addressing, might very well have experienced persecution themselves, particularly the persecution of Emperor Nero. One of the complications of that persecution was that a number of the Christians began squealing on the others—rather like today, when if you capture a lower-ranking member of the Mafia, you promise him security and immunity if he will squeal on the others. This threw the Christian community into consternation, because they no longer could just gather together and feel the comfort of one another. In an atmosphere of spying and betrayal, you don't know whom you can trust. You don't know who is going to hand in your name and reveal what you said—so the comfort of the group was lost.

It's also possible, some scholars say, that the author of this gospel, traditionally St. Mark, had experienced the destruction of the Temple of Jerusalem in the year 70. This was a total catastrophe for the Jewish people and the early Christians. We don't have anything comparable today in importance to the Temple for those people, whether politically, religiously, or even economically. The Temple was the center of Judaism in a way that St. Peter's Basilica does not equal.

When the Temple was destroyed, the Jews were really thrown into confusion—and when things like that happen, people have different ideas about what to do to regroup, or come back, or whom to follow. So the persecution literature provides some kind of hope and guidance to people in their pain, their fear for themselves and their families, their suspicion and resentment, and their false hopes.

This discourse of Our Lord, too, is aimed at that, and when Jesus comes to the end he says simply, "Stay awake!" This is a challenge. You have to accept the fact that the command has a special significance because these words are Our Lord's final words to his disciples, and they bear quite a few different meanings. I'm going to offer one, but I want to suggest most of all that it's up to each of us to think about what this could mean. What does it mean if Jesus says to you, "Stay awake"?

Keeping Awake

What is the sleep? And what is being awake? In a few weeks, we celebrate the birth of Christ. While we are all aware of the coming of Christmas, each of us has a different receptivity for Christ. We all honor him, respect him, etc., but he gets into people's hearts and lives to different degrees. He has a different significance for different people. For some people he's peripheral, for some people he means a lot, and for some people he means everything. I cannot tell, when Christmas comes around, who will be most receptive, who will be most awake to let him in.

At the time of Our Lord, when he was walking around Galilee, all sorts of people saw and heard him. Some of them really let him in; they gave up everything, changed their whole lives; he became the center of their lives. Other people gave him encouragement to heal somebody. For some people there was no great impact; they didn't let him in much. Of course, others were persecuting him.

How awake are *you* to let him in? Whether on December 25th or whenever he comes, is not *now* a better time for Christ and his wisdom and love to enter in some real, tangible way into your life?

Suppose Christ were up at Aspen. What would people make of him? Some people would point him out, like you point out a movie star, and other people would take advantage of it and let him in. If he came around and he needed a room, and he knocked on your door and said, "Do you have a spare room here, I need a place to stay?" you might say, "Well, no we don't. As a matter of fact we do, but my husband and I…I suggest you try over there." Wouldn't this be the blunder of blunders, as it was for people in Our Lord's time, to let that opportunity pass by? They weren't doing it consciously; it wasn't exactly sinful, it was just stupid. They had so much, it was right there.

This is an issue for Christmas because our culture knows Christmas as a big selling season of gifts. Three-quarters of the toys in this country are sold within these few weeks. There's a nice dinner and so on. But how do we let him in? What would that be like? What does that mean to us? How much have we let him in already, and how much more could we let him in, and how would we go about it, what would it mean? It's a very personal thing. That's one level, letting Christ in, being awake and not asleep, awake to that opportunity. But there's another level.

Yesterday I was at Glenwood, visiting some friends who had come for Thanksgiving to visit with their daughter and her children, who are twin girls, born last Christmas. They're a year old, and they are a delight. They were crawling around on the floor in perpetual motion, the two of them, just lovely as can be, happy, with big eyes, and the grandmother was crazy about them. She was fascinated, out of herself with love for them, and the grandfather was down on the floor, crawling around and making faces with them. I brought them three jars of jelly, and the twins were rolling them around the floor and tearing off the labels—just a perfect delight. It reminded me of several years ago when we had two puppies at the monastery. They were so much fun that every single monk, every night, after supper, would go out to the back porch to play with those puppies and watch them play. They were irresistible.

Those twin girls showed up a year ago as God's Word, God's gift. Do they belong to the parents, or do they belong to God? They showed up in the middle of that family, and the family has never been the same. They kept the parents awake for the past year, but they've also pulled out love and responsibility from those parents. They have grown the parents up, and brought joy that the parents never knew before, as well as pain. The parents see the preciousness. But *everybody's* precious; every single person is God's child—yet we're asleep. We see other people's shortcomings; we don't see that they're precious, they come from God. We're not awake to that.

One day, in the 1950s in my monastery in Spencer, Massachusetts, one of the brothers picked up a hitchhiker, and the hitchhiker pulled a gun on him and took the car. The brother never saw the car again, as far as I can recall. The next Sunday the abbot giving his talk said, "I want to make it clear now, I don't want any of you picking up hitchhikers. It's too dangerous." I don't know what happened in the heads of other people, but in my head that became the law. That was the injunction: Don't pick up hitchhikers. In 1961 that abbot retired, so he was no longer my authority, but I still carried out his injunction. Then, some years later, he was dead and I was still carrying this injunction of his, passing hitchhikers right by as if I was asleep. I didn't even notice, it had nothing to do with me.

Then, a few years ago, the pastor up in Aspen got sick, so I had to take his masses on Saturday afternoon and Sunday, and the gospel was the story of the good Samaritan. In that story this poor fellow is beaten up, is lying on the ground, and guess who comes by first? The priest. He's on his way back from the Temple, and he passes him by, he doesn't notice. And who comes second? The Levite. A Levite is like a deacon. And he passes him by. He doesn't notice. And the third person is the Samaritan—an outsider.

I was driving back from Saturday afternoon mass, and there was a hitchhiker. All of a sudden I *saw* him. I was *awake*. I picked him up, and I explained to him why I had to pick him up. I was too embarrassed to do otherwise; I was a priest passing him by.

This is an example of being asleep or awake, noticing. Christ, in his last words to his apostles, wanted to mention that you don't *know* when God is going to show up. You don't know what He's going to be wearing, what the voice sounds like, the expression on the face, the color of the skin. You know you don't like the looks of him, you know he doesn't sing very well, or smell very good, or dress very well, etc. But Jesus teaches his disciples and us to have a heart like his, and to let him in—to really let him into our hearts and our life—is to get that way yourself. When you're doing that he is proud of you. But notice how often you fall asleep. You go back to sleep, get into your little bed, and don't hear or see anything. You dream that you are the center of the world. We all do this, so it's a challenge to every one of us to stay awake. Don't go back to sleep. Stay awake. You never know when God is going to show up.

Waiting on God

JOSEPH BOYLE

The Second Sunday of Advent

The beginning of the good news about Jesus Christ, the Son of God. It is written in the book of the prophet Isaiah, "Look, I am going to send my messenger before you. He will prepare your way. A voice cries in the wilderness, 'Prepare a way for the Lord. Make his path straight.' "And so it was that John the Baptist appeared in the wilderness, proclaiming a baptism of repentance for the forgiveness of sins. All Judea and all the people of Jerusalem made their way to him; as they were baptized by him in the River Jordan they confessed their sins. John wore a garment of camel-skin, and he lived on locusts and wild honey. In the course of his preaching he said, "Someone is following me, someone who is more powerful than I am, and I am not fit to kneel and undo the strap of his sandals. I have baptized you with water, but he will baptize you with the Holy Spirit." (Mark 1:1–8)

On this day, the second Sunday of Advent, the message is clear: Prepare a way for the Lord. We hear it in the beginning of the Gospel of Mark, where Mark quotes Isaiah. And this ties in very neatly with the Gospel of the previous chapter on staying awake.

Now, added to "stay awake" is the concept "be prepared." Prepare yourself: prepare a way for the Lord. To bring this message across, the Church brings in front of us in the reading that starts this chapter one of the most colorful characters in the whole Bible—John the Baptist. John comes up out of the wilderness, the desert, perhaps an associate of the community of the Essenes, wearing an outfit of camel skins and eating locusts, his hair totally unkempt—at least that is the artist's picture in my mind for John.

John is a very powerful fellow with a very powerful message, and he is absolutely unmistakable. When I try to come up with some kind of a likeness, all I can think of is our own Father Theophane. He is also singular in appearance and unmistakable. I sometimes get a phone call from somebody who is coming to the retreat house and needs to be picked up at the airport. I tell him that Father Theophane will be picking him up and the visitor will ask, "How will I recognize him? Will he have a sign like 'Little Nell,' or 'Silver Tree Inn,' or 'Saint Benedict's'?" I tell him, "Believe me, when you get to the airport and you look around you will know who is picking you up from the monastery. You may not want to ride with him, but you'll know who's doing it!"

That is the way I see it with John the Baptist. The gospel tells us that all of Jerusalem goes out to see him. Clearly, there is no need to ask how he will be recognized. It is obvious. And John is a hard act to follow. It is a challenge for us to come along and say, "Here we are, two thousand years later, and we need to take this message to heart and say to ourselves: 'Prepare a way for the Lord.' "

What does it mean in this day and age to prepare a way for the Lord? Since we are in the context of the liturgy of Advent moving toward Christmas, we are thinking about Christmas. We are thinking about the mystery of Christmas as an encounter with the Christ, as a deepening of our union with him, and opening the heart. This is what, it seems to me, Christmas is, and all the generosity that flows at Christmastime is about opening the heart in the light of Christ and his grace, and encountering him more deeply.

The question is: How completely are we prepared to enter into this grace? How do we open ourselves? What do we do? There are, I imagine, any number of answers, and none of them is better than another. However, the answer I want to pursue is this: In the midst of our very busy days, especially before Christmas, we need to find some time of quiet, where we can reflect, be still, go inside, and pray with a kind of prayer that reaches deep inside us. At this time, we should get in touch with the inner hunger and deep desire of the heart, so that when Christ comes—who answers that deep desire of our heart—we are down in that place that can receive him and open to the flow of grace.

My suggestion, however, comes with a warning: If we choose to do this, it is an act of war against our culture. Our culture hates silence, quiet, waiting—all the words we associate with Advent. Instead, our culture gives us more and more ways to fill in our time. There is entertainment and the Internet—we no longer have to go out of our house to be able to watch anything in the world. Besides entertainment there is simply our work, our responsibilities, our connections, the things we have to maintain. For many of the people I know, work is what generates most of the push on activity, and most of the guilt feelings we have if we slow down. We are always telling ourselves that once we finish the task at hand we will be quiet, etc. We find it so hard not to fill in our time, to tell ourselves that waiting and being quiet are not a waste of time.

Modern conveniences have created a situation where we never have to sit still and wait to do something. I was stuck in rush-hour traffic recently; we were brought to a standstill for a few minutes. I happened to look at the car ahead to see what the driver was doing with the wait. Naturally, he was on a car phone and I began to think to myself that if I had a mini-cassette recorder I could have been getting notes down for this homily. Neither of us could abide the thought of just being quiet and waiting until we could move.

Thus, there are an infinite number of things we can be doing; and I am not against any of those devices that enable the efficient, productive use of our time. I simply want to make it known that, in the middle of all of the noise and distraction of work and entertainment, our culture has totally devalued silence, waiting, and simply staying open to quiet.

How hard this is for me, for instance, comes out in two similar incidents that happened recently. In the first incident, I was doing a directed retreat, working on a scripture text, and I reached a point of real inner quiet. However, I felt ready to move on to the next text and when I checked in with the retreat director, the director had to say, "Stop! Where are you going? What are you going on to another text for? Just stay with the silence." I was geared to do something else, to move on, to get on with the retreat.

In the second, I was at a workshop where there was significant sharing going on, and at one point I expressed some experiences from my youth. It was very powerful, and I suppose even some of my emotion showed. After I had finished, somebody else started talking and I started listening. One of the staff members came over and sat beside me, "Hey, let that go," the staff member said. "Stay with your feelings." My mental orientation rebelled at that. After all, weren't we in a workshop? Weren't we meant to listen to one another? Wasn't that what it was all about? Didn't I have a responsibility to be part of this whole thing? It took an outside reminder telling me to stay with my own feelings for me to acknowledge those feelings and let them be present to me. To do that I had to silence the other stuff coming in.

This "other stuff" is what we are up against when we prepare ourselves for silence, waiting, and readiness. If we are honest, that "stuff" is not just what culture impinges upon us from without. It comes from within, too. For instance, suppose you hear yourself saying, "This afternoon I'm going to take twenty minutes of silence. I'm just going to sit still, not even read, just be still." Unfortunately, when you close your eyes, you tend to find that the Lord does not come strolling up and say, "Hi, I'm really glad you've taken this time. I've been wanting to talk to you. I have several things: I want to tell you how good you are and how much I love you!" And so on. Once in a while in prayer we get an experience somewhat like that, but it is not very often.

Most of the time, for most of us, when we take that time of silence and quiet, we sit still and the distractions come and we let them go. When we get down to emptiness, to those parts of ourselves that are incomplete, to the deep hunger inside, the desire and longing, it is not very pleasant. In these situations, we don't need a push from the culture outside us; we ourselves are ready to leave at that point. We think, "Hmm, aren't the Denver Broncos doing something about now? Maybe they need some prayer." Or, if we are a tad more subtle, we might say, "Geez, maybe I should make some notes about this emptiness. It could come in helpful for a future homily." We do anything we can *not* to stay with the experience.

Staying with the Experience

How do we change ourselves so that we do stay with the experience—the experience, as I say, that will bring us to the hunger and desire within us? An eloquent preacher or writer can make hunger sound desirable and good. However, when we experience it, that hunger is just hunger. It doesn't feel so good, so we tend to exit.

Sometimes, when we see that hunger in other people, it looks good and we can recognize it and say, "Wow, there's suffering and there's pain in there but isn't it incredible that they're at that deep level, and they're moving spiritually?" But we ourselves are not experiencing what they are experiencing. We are only seeing it from outside.

I remember an instance of this at World Youth Day in the early 1990s. Denver was chosen as the city where young people from all over the world would gather and be addressed by the Pope. The people of Denver didn't have complete consensus about whether this event was going to be a good thing for the city. Some felt that the traffic was bad enough without having a huge event such as the World Youth Day. Then there was the issue of who was going to pay for the clean-up.

When the time finally arrived, however, the experience was nice, edifying, and inspiring. People were impressed with these youngsters. Instead of the crime rate for the week going up, as many had feared it would, it went down. For some of the people I talked to who were actually closer to what was happening and were involved in the event, what appeared particularly strong was these young people's hunger for the spiritual. That hunger probably didn't make them feel good, and yet we could recognize it for what is was and say, "Yes, that's what makes a life work, that's what makes life go deep, that's what will really be of value."

We have to make that apply to ourselves. We have to hold on to the hunger and allow it to open us so that when Christ comes with the graces of Christmas, of transformation, of opening our hearts, we are ready, in a deep place, and the transformation is not a superficial thing that just touches lightly and passes us by. We need to acknowledge that going to the quiet and reflective place in us is not an escape, but an engagement.

As Christians, clearly we have giant obligations—to be the presence of Christ, to take care of the needy, to respond to the physically hungry and poor, and so on. That is clearly who we are as Christians. Yet, when I hear, "Prepare a way for the Lord," what resonates for me is that we need to take the time to be quiet, still, and alone with ourselves.

This is not a contradiction. If we really get quiet and meet the Lord at that place of quiet, then we have the love and the Christ-heart to bring to the world. Without that love, we try merely to do the things that Christ says. We read the Sermon on the Mount and attempt to put the principles into practice. But without that inner contact our efforts tend to be short-lived and half-hearted. The energy source, the interior resource, dries up and disappears; or else our ego gets into the practice and we begin to deviate because it is our ego and power needs that are being tapped and not the grace of Christ. If, however, we have that combination of going within to realize our hunger and our need and our openness to receive that grace, then we will have the ability to be a loving presence in the world.

This dual expression is what I see modeled in Jesus' own life. Jesus clearly was a man for others, going outward, caring for the needy wherever he met them. Yet he constantly moved inwards and took that time of solitude. He often went off by himself for the whole night—alone, praying, renewing from within.

To me, then, Advent has something of the quality of those nights when Jesus prayed. I see Advent in the liturgical season as a time to pull back. We should take a five- or ten-minute period, or any moment that comes, and be quiet, open to the Lord, be receptive, staying on when all of our stuff goes marching by us. By staying, we are receptive to the graces that Christ brings us. When we do this, Advent becomes a wonderful time, inviting us in. We can say to our culture, "All right, we have our entertainment and work, and we're part of it. But I also deeply need this inner space." This is my invitation to you and, I believe, the Church's invitation. Indeed, I think I can go further back to the Psalmist and hand you an invitation from God, "Be still and know that I am God" (Psalms 46:10).

It is hard to know God without stillness. Granted sometimes he overwhelms us in the midst of our noise—clearly God has infinite power. At the same time, for most people, we need to take that time of stillness so that God can draw us into our deeper part and meet us there.

3

The Kingdom is Love

THEOPHANE BOYD

The Third Sunday of Advent

A man came, sent by God; his name was John. He came as a witness, a witness to speak for the light, so that everyone might believe through him. He was not the light, only a witness to speak for the light.

This is how John appeared as a witness. When the Jews sent priests and Levites from Jerusalem to ask him, "Who are you?" he not only declared, but he declared quite openly, "I am not the Christ." "Well then," they said, "Are you Elijah?" "I am not," he said. "Are you the prophet?" He answered, "No." And so they said to him, "Who are you? We must take back an answer to those who sent us. What have you to say about yourself?" So John said, "I am, as Isaiah prophesied, a voice that cries in the wilderness, 'Make a straight way for the Lord.' "

Now these men had been sent by the Pharisees, and they put the further question to him, "Why are you baptizing if you are not the Christ and not Elijah and not the prophet?" And John replied, "I baptize with water, but there stands among you, unknown to you, the one who is coming after me, and I am not fit to undo his sandal strap." This happened in Bethany on the far side of the Jordan where John was baptizing. (John 1:6–8, 19–28)

It is Christmas in a week and a half, and here we are ritualizing early in order to stir up our receptivity. That's the big issue—our receptivity. At Christmas, or at any mass communion time, we all receive the same communion, but who is most receptive, who swallows the Lord whole? It makes all the difference in the world. Thus, last week and this week, we speak about John the Baptist.

The scholars say that John the Baptist had so impressed the people with his fasting and austerities, his obvious holiness, that he was in danger of upstaging Jesus. This is why the evangelists were at pains to have him say that Christ is greater than he is. Although this text was composed forty or fifty or more years after Christ had gone, the evangelists still felt a need to spread the message that Christ is greater than John the Baptist. So John says here, "Well, I just baptize with water. I'm not the Messiah; I'm not even fit to undo his sandal strap." All the gospels have the same kind of testimony. Jesus himself admits the greatness of John when he says, "Among those born of woman, no one is greater than John." Yet, Jesus says, "The least in the kingdom of God is greater than he."

Preachers have struggled with that paradox. What does that mean— "the least in the kingdom of God is greater than he"? Does it mean that whoever you pour water on is greater than John the Baptist? I think the statement refers to whoever really enters into the kingdom that he talks about—that's the great theme of Christ in the synoptic gospels—the kingdom of God, or the kingdom of heaven, as St. Matthew calls it. It's the vision of Christ, the world he lived in, and John the Baptist is the summit of the whole Jewish tradition. All the great holy ones and prophets in the Jewish tradition are all heading toward him. He will be the great prophet who, with his own finger, can point to the Messiah, the Christ, and thereby the coming of the kingdom. It's not simply that Christ is greater than any of them, but that Christ will usher in a whole new ballgame, the kingdom of God. I think we should probably have a whole year in which the theme of all the gospels is just that— what does the kingdom of God, the kingdom of heaven mean? But we're falling asleep on it, we've heard it so many times.

Once when I was strolling through the Magic Monastery I came across a building with a sign outside that said "The House of Perfect Love." Now, don't ask me why I didn't go in. I didn't even look in. I hurried past. The next day, when I was leaving the Magic Monastery, I was going down the hill and I went over to give some money to a beggar, and the beggar said to me, "Why are you weeping?"

I said, "Me? I'm not weeping." He said, "Oh, you're not weeping on the outside, you're weeping on the inside." It was true. I was weeping inside because I had not been man enough to go into that House of Perfect Love. When I admitted this to the beggar, he said, "I understand. My own name used to be Fear, and I know that sometimes you can't manage to get into that magic house. But then perhaps you can get into the *real* house of perfect love. Sometimes it's the other way around. You can get into a magic house, but you can't get into the real house. Here, why don't you sit down next to me and take my hand? Together we'll go into the real house of perfect love. People won't suspect a thing. They'll just think we're beggars, and they'll look down on us, and they'll give us their money." God bless that beggar.

What is it like in the house of perfect love? What do you expect? What do you think it would be like? Do you think everybody there would be charitable? Do you think they'd appreciate the good things you do, your intelligence, and so on? If you go to mass in India, when you come out after mass you find beggars lined up, perhaps six or eight on one side and four or five on the other side—a dreadful sight, because they have leprosy, their faces are disfigured and their hands gnarled, or they lack a leg or an arm, or they're blind, and so on. As you leave mass, you go over and give them some coins. I remember thinking one time that perhaps one of them had found his way into the house of perfect love. I may be a bishop, or a monk, or a priest; I may be learned, intelligent, have all the social graces. But the beggar may have found his way into the house of perfect love.

Many people are fascinated with the image of John the Baptist even today. I remember reading one time that there are more churches—and, until recently, more boys—named after John the Baptist in the world than any other saint. It's John the Baptist, not the Evangelist, who has caught people's imagination. Some people, when they see someone like me, who looks emaciated, think I must be holy. But it's about the kingdom of God, not who worships Christ, who goes to church on Sunday, or who keeps away from sins of the flesh. It's the kingdom of God, God's vision, God's way of looking at things, God's values, the house of perfect love.

The Presentation

WILLIAM MENINGER

The Feast of the Presentation

When the day came for them to be purified as laid down by the Law of Moses, the parents of Jesus took him up to Jerusalem to present him to the Lord—observing what stands written in the Law, "Every first-born male must be consecrated to the Lord"—and also to offer in sacrifice, in accordance with what is said in the Law, "a pair of turtledoves or two young pigeons." Now in Jerusalem there was a man named Simeon. He was an upright and devout man; he looked forward to Israel's comforting, and the Holy Spirit rested on him. It had been revealed to him by the Holy Spirit that he would not see death until he had set eyes on the Christ of the Lord. Prompted by the Spirit he came to the Temple; and when the parents brought in the child Jesus to do for him what the Law required, he took him into his arms and blessed God; and said, "Now, Master, you can let your servant go in peace just as you promised; because my eyes have seen the salvation which you have prepared for all the nations to see; a light to enlighten the pagans and the glory of your people Israel."

As the child's father and mother stood there wondering at the things that were being said about him, Simeon blessed them and said to Mary his mother, "You see this child, he is destined for the fall and for the rising of many in Israel, destined to be a sign that is rejected, and a sword will pierce your own soul, too, so that the secret thoughts of many may be laid bare."

There was a prophetess, also, Anna the daughter of Phanuel of the tribe of Asher. She was well on in years. Her days of girlhood over, she had been married for seven years before becoming a widow. She was now eighty-four years old and never left the Temple, serving God night and day with fasting and prayer. She came by just at that moment and began to praise God; and she spoke of the child to all who looked forward to the deliverance of Jerusalem. When they had done everything the Law of the Lord required, they went back to Galilee, to their own town of Nazareth. Meanwhile, the child grew to maturity, and he was filled with wisdom; and God's favor was with him. (Luke 2:22–40)

If you were to visit our refectory after mass this mornmg you would find something that is quite surprising. We still have our Christmas tree! Somebody claimed that we do this because one of our monks cries when we take it down. But that is not the real reason. The real reason is that the Christmas season actually extends up until today. Today, February 2nd, is liturgically the end of the Christmas season, the Feast of the Presentation; it is, as it were, on this day that we remove the Christ child from his crib and carry him to the Temple to begin his work. And his first work is to be taken in the arms of his mother and father to be presented to God.

The first reading this morning was followed by the majestic Psalm 24, "Oh gates lift high your heads, rise you ancient doors, let the King of Glory in" (v. 7). This was originally written for the triumphant entrance into Solomon's Temple of the Ark of the Covenant after it was returned to Jerusalem. The Ark had been used to lead the armies of Judea into a military victory, so its return was a glorious, triumphant re-entry of God into his Holy of Holies. It was believed that the Ark had actually grown physically, so that the doors of the Temple could no longer accommodate it. In the song of praise an appeal was made to the arches of the doorways to rise up, grow bigger, and enable the God of Glory, dwelling in the Ark, to enter the place of His repose.

It is a marvelous scene: the array of Levites (the deacons of the synagogue), the rows upon rows of priests, maidens with instruments, dancing, and then the king leading his generals and the heroes of his army. Finally, carried on the shoulders of four priests is the Ark of the Covenant, the seat of God's glory, brought into the Temple to be placed in the Holy of Holies, where God would again dwell among His people. And accompanying this, all the people singing "let the King of Glory in." Who is the King of Glory? It is the Lord, strong and valiant in battle. He is the King of Glory.

In today's gospel reading the Church gives us quite a different picture. The same victorious psalm is chanted, but we look in vain for priests, soldiers, dancing maidens, and rejoicing crowds. Instead, we see a small, simple family: Joseph, a tradesman, carrying in his hand a wooden cage with two pigeons, and his young wife, Mary, carrying their infant son to present him to the Lord as required by the law. Any singing of glorious psalms will have to wait a long time, until the Church, reflecting on this mystery of the Presentation, sees with the eyes of faith in this small family God entering the Temple in the arms of his mother, and hears with the ears of faith angelic choirs filling the heavenly vaults with their singing, "Rise you ancient doors, it is the King of Glory."

In contrast, it is very interesting to note the site of the birth of Jesus in Bethlehem. This place, the oldest church in the world, has a door so small that in order to get through it, you have to bend over and enter on your knees. Visitors are forced to be humble to enter the place of Jesus' birth. However, in today's liturgy, when Christ is brought to his Father's home, the very gates themselves are told to rise up in order to accommodate his greatness.

I would like to change the picture again. This time it is the Aspen Hospital, and the maternity ward that I passed after visiting a sick monk. As I approached the door I saw standing by it a young man holding his newborn son. He said not a word but looked up at me as I was passing by. I didn't know him, but the look in his eyes summoned me over, and he drew me into the aura of his silent rejoicing, his song of pride, his gratitude, awe, and love for the newborn child he held in his arms. I was literally forced to stop, admire the child, and congratulate the proud father.

This very simple, human, but powerful event gives meaning to the feast we celebrate today, the Feast of the Presentation. It conjures up a picture of two people carrying a newborn child. We do not need to hear the drums and the cymbals and the singing; we do not need to see the priests, the soldiers, the dancers, or the celebrating crowds. We can find the meaning of this feast, I think, if we look into the outreaching arms of a small group of people: this young man and his baby, Mary and Joseph with theirs—as the scriptures say—the arms of the upright and devout, Simeon, and then in the arms of the prophetess, Anna. We then have to ask ourselves: How do we hold the Christ child in *our* arms? How do we hold the Christ child as Mary and Joseph did, and draw others to him? How do we mother and protect Jesus, as his parents did, and present him to God according to the law?

We do this as we take on in compassion and love whatever and whoever God places in our arms. I am sure you remember the song that goes, "He's got the whole world in his hands,/the whole wide world in his hands." Well, this world is given to us and we are the ones who have it in our hands. We each have our own segment of it, as well as its entirety. We are called to nourish and to protect it, and return it to the Lord. This means we nourish and cherish not only those who have been given to us—our children, the flesh of our flesh—but also the very least of our brothers and sisters whom we may recognize only in their cries for help in this global village we call a world. As Joseph and Mary observed the Jewish law, the law we observe when we do this is the law of Jesus, "Whatever you do to one of these, the least of my brothers, you do to me" (Matthew 25:40).

This is how we hold the Christ child in our arms, as Mary and Joseph did, and draw others to him. This is how we hold the child Jesus in our arms as Simeon and Anna did and draw others to us. We rejoice, like them, in the reality of Jesus in our lives. We permit Jesus to be real. In Protestant terminology, we *acknowledge* him as our personal Savior. We seek to take all of that genuine love we have received in our lives as a reflection of God and endeavor to extend that love daily to our personal worlds and the entire world. We accept the duties, responsibilities, cares, and crosses of our lives, or, as Simeon explained it to Mary, the swords which will pierce our very souls (and such swords are inevitable for anyone who would carry the Christ child). We accept them and we transform them with love because we confess with joy, as Simeon did, that our eyes have seen the salvation that God has promised in the victory that this child has won for us, and which we claim as our own.

Finally, we hold the child Jesus in our arms as the prophetess Anna did, and draw others into our aura. Anna praised God, and she spoke of the child to all who looked forward to the deliverance of Jerusalem. The Christ in our lives, the Christ in our arms, is to be loved and in that loving to be shared, even as that young man at Aspen Hospital did and even as Mary and Joseph did. Finally, as the body of Christ, we are also that child, presented to the Father, with pride, joy, gratitude, and love. And so, today is our day too, the Feast of our Presentation.

The Victory

The First Sunday of Lent

The Spirit drove Jesus out into the wilderness, and
he remained there for forty days, and was tempted
by Satan. He was with the wild beasts, and the
angels looked after him. After John had been arrest-
ed, Jesus went into Galilee. There he proclaimed the
good news from God. "The time has come," he
said, "and the kingdom of God is close at hand.
Repent, and believe the good news." (Mark
1:12–15)

I have had the privilege and pleasure, as a spiritual director, of leading a number of tours to the Holy Land. One
of the things that I like in taking people around Israel is a
trip to the top of the Mount of Olives. Riding up to the
very summit of the Mount of Olives, even sitting in the
bus, you can see both sides of the mountain. On one side,

to the west, is the city of Jerusalem, including the ancient walled city. On the other side, to the East, you get a spectacular view of the wilderness of Judea. It is quite a contrast: a stark, desert area covered with low, brown sand dunes without vegetation stretching into the distance, ending nine miles away in Jericho, which your imagination almost sees. This is the place where the Spirit, as Mark says, "drove Jesus out into the wilderness."

The language that Mark uses is very strong. This account of Jesus' temptation is also found in Matthew and Luke, but in Mark the version is quite different. In Matthew and Luke it says, "Jesus was *led* by the Spirit" (Matthew 4:1 and Luke 4:2). The word "led" is gentle, inoffensive, without any particular strain or stress. However, the word that Mark uses is "drove."

Being a student of the scriptures, I know that when I see something like this there is something special behind it, so I have to look until I find what that is. And find it I did.

Driven into the Wilderness
On the feast of the Holy Day of Yom Kippur, the Day of Atonement, it was the custom of the Jews to gather together at the Temple, where the High Priest would read out a list of the sins of the people. After each sin the people would say something like, "Lord, have mercy on us." Then, symbolically, the priest would take those sins in his hands, and he would place his hands on the head of a goat. This symbolized that all of the sins of the people were now imposed on this goat, who was known, not surprisingly, as

the *scape*goat. The priests would then drive it into the wilderness of Judea, presumably to die in the desert, and, with its death, take their sins away.

This is what Mark is telling us by his statement "The Spirit drove Jesus out into the wilderness." Jesus is our scapegoat. Jesus is our sacrifice. Jesus is the one who took the burden of our sins. Somehow or other, what Jesus did then was done for the people—that is for us—when the Spirit drove him out into the desert.

What, according to Matthew, Mark, and Luke, was actually done? The answer is that Jesus was tempted. He was tested. He was tried by Satan. He did not die at that moment. Instead, he was tested and tempted. Now, St. Paul tells us that Jesus never sinned, that he was like us in everything except sin. But if he was like us in everything except sin, then that means that Jesus really could be tempted. It was a real temptation, and not some kind of artificial charade. Indeed, this trial that we hear in the gospel today would be meaningless if it were not real.

I think the statement, "The Spirit drove Jesus out into the wilderness," indicates on the part of Jesus a certain reluctance. He did not want to do this; he had to be driven. It seems that only after he underwent this trial and overcame these temptations could he then be free to proclaim the Good News that the kingdom of God was at hand. Once more, we need to look, as it were, between the lines and behind the text that St. Mark has given us.

Besides being a scapegoat and taking out into the desert the sins of the people, Jesus was recapitulating in himself the entire people of God. He was symbolically repeating their historical experience to show its real meaning. The children of Israel were in the desert for forty years until they were ready for the promised land, the kingdom of God. So Jesus was in the desert for forty days, and only when this had come about—with the assistance of God through the help of his angels, as they ministered to the Jewish people—was he able to bring us to the kingdom.

When he left the wilderness of Judea, Jesus went to Galilee and proclaimed the nearness of the kingdom of God. "Repent and believe; because the kingdom of God is at hand" (Mark 1:14). This time, however, the kingdom of God was not the tiny land of Israel, but the very portals of heaven itself.

Mark, in his account of the temptation of Jesus, does not list the temptations as Matthew and Luke do. There are three temptations; Jesus is challenged to turn stones into bread, to throw himself from the pinnacle of the Temple, and to fall down and worship Satan with the promise that all the kingdoms of the world will be his. A lot has been said about these temptations, and rightly so. However, Mark's concern is not so much what these temptations were but the fact that they happened.

This is where you and I come into the picture. These temptations are our temptations. In the same way that the scapegoat bore the sins of the Jews, so Jesus carried our sins, and his temptations are ours. Jesus underwent them for our sake, Mark is telling us something very real, concrete, and significant in our daily lives. He is telling us that Jesus won the battle and the victory for us.

Here at the monastery, we post on our bulletin board the many letters and requests for prayers that we receive from people. Once there was a particularly poignant one from someone who seemed to be almost in despair, begging for prayers, and trying to see some light at the end of a dark tunnel. What this person needed, and what, hopefully, our prayers helped this person understand, is that there is no place for despair because there is no place for defeat. Jesus has won, for us, the victory. It has been achieved.

In Matthew, the text says the Devil left Jesus and angels appeared and looked after him. Luke, however, says something a little more ominous, that we also have to face: he says the Devil left him, to return at the appointed time (Luke 4:3). So, while the victory was won, there is something in it that is not totally decisive. And that something is our own freedom and commitment, and the necessity for us, in faith, to reach out and grasp that victory. However, in order to do this, we have to experience this temptation. It has to be translated into our own lives.

What are your temptations? Sometimes the three temptations of Jesus are put into sort of generic classifications that we all have to deal with. So, the first temptation is for food and security; the second is to be cared for; and the third is the lust for earthly possessions. Nevertheless, one of the things that we have to remember, especially in spiritual counseling, when somebody talks about the temptations or trials they are undergoing and expresses shame about them, is that no one should ever be ashamed of temptation. Temptations are not sins. Temptations are trials. Temptations are a call to virtue, something that is given to strengthen us so we can reaffirm our commitments to God. We should never be ashamed of temptations. We should only be ashamed when we give in to them. We are to be assured in this gospel that Jesus died for us, he died for our sins, and he rose for our justification. Thus, we need to reach out and claim the victory, but realize it will be a trial and temptation for us. Satan will reappear at the appointed time. But we need to remember that angels will minister to us. We will have God's help and his grace.

It is in this spirit that we are to move forward during this season of Lent, as we progress toward the new light, the heavenly kingdom promised us on Easter Sunday. We have an angel, a messenger from God, and our very angel is Jesus himself. St. Paul, in the Epistle to the Romans, reminds us of this very graphically. He says, "With God on our side, who can be against us? (8:31)" God did not spare his own Son, but gave him up to benefit us all; can anyone condemn when God acquits? Jesus not only died for us, he rose from the dead, and at God's right hand he stands and pleads for us.

6

The Light of the World

WILLIAM MENINGER

The Fourth Sunday of Lent

As [Jesus] walked along, he saw a man blind from birth. His disciples asked him, "Rabbi, who sinned, this man or his parents, that he was born blind?" Jesus answered, "Neither this man nor his parents sinned. He was born blind so that God's works might be revealed in him. We must work the works of Him who sent me while it is day. Night is coming when no one can work. As long as I am in the world I am the Light of the World."

When he had said this, he spat on the ground and made mud with the saliva, and spread the mud on the man's eyes, saying to him, "Go, wash in the Pool of Siloam." Then he went and washed and came back able to see.

The neighbors and those who had seen him before as a beggar began to ask, "Is this not the man who used to sit and beg?" Some were saying, "It is he." Others were saying, "No, but it is someone like him." He kept saying, "I am the man." But they kept asking him, "Then how were your eyes opened?" He answered, "The man called Jesus made mud, spread it on my eyes, and said to me: 'Go to Siloam and wash.' Then I went, and washed, and received my sight." They said to him, "Where is he?" He said, "I do not know."

They brought to the Pharisees the man who had formerly been blind. Now it was a Sabbath day when Jesus made the mud and opened his eyes. Then the Pharisees also began to ask him how he had received his sight. He said to them, "He put mud on my eyes, then I washed, and now I see." Some of the Pharisees said, "This man is not from God, for he does not observe the Sabbath." But others said, "How can man who is a sinner perform such signs?" And they were divided.

So they said again to the blind man, "What do you say about him, it was your eyes he opened?" And he said, "He is a prophet."

The Jews did not believe that he had been blind and had received his sight until they called the parents of the man who had received his sight, and asked them, "Is this your son who you say was born blind? How then does he now see?" His parents answered, "We know that this is our son and that he was born blind, but we do not know how it is that he sees, nor do we know who opened his eyes. Ask him, he is of age. He will speak for himself." His parents said this because they were afraid of the Jews, for the Jews had already agreed that anyone who confessed Jesus to be the Messiah would be put out of the synagogue. Therefore, his parents said, "He is of age; ask him."

So for the second time, they called the man who had been blind and they said to him, "Give glory to God! We know that this man is a sinner." He answered, "I do not know whether he is a sinner. One thing I do know is that though I was blind now I see." They said to him, "What did he do to you? How did he open your eyes?" He answered them, "I have told you already and you would not listen. Why do you want to hear it again? Do you also want to become his disciples?"

Then they reviled him, saying, "You are his disciple, but we are disciples of Moses: we know that God has spoken to Moses, but as for this man, we do not know where he comes from." The man answered, "Here is an astonishing thing. You do not know where he comes from and yet he opened my eyes! We know that God does not listen to sinners, but He does listen to one who worships Him and obeys His will. Never since the world began has it been heard that anyone opened the eyes of a person born blind. If this man were not from God, he could do nothing." They answered him, "You were

born entirely in sin, and are you trying to teach us!"
And they drove him out.

Jesus heard that they had driven him out, and
when he found him he said, "Do you believe in the
Son of Man?" He answered, "And who is he, sir?
Tell me so that I may believe in him." Jesus said to
him, "You have seen him; and the one speaking
with you is he." He said, "Lord, I believe," and he
worshipped him.

Jesus said, "I came into this world for judgment,
so that those who do not see may see, and those do
see may become blind." Some of the Pharisees near
him heard this and said, "Surely we are not blind,
are we?" Jesus said to them, "If you were blind, you
would not have sinned, but now that you say, 'we
see,' your sin remains." (John 9:1–41)

O ne of the interpretations of this fascinating gospel
passage is that it is an anticipation of Easter, and in a
very real sense it is actually an invitation to take part in the
Easter vigil service. This will be plain in a moment. The
gospel begins with the apostles apparently walking around
the Temple area asking Jesus a question. They see a blind
man begging, and in the typical way of disciples to a guru,
or rabbi, they introduce a theological issue. So they ask
him, "Rabbi, who sinned, this man or his parents?"

This question presupposes that somebody, somewhere,
sinned, or this man would not be blind. In other words,
blindness is the result of sin. The Pharisees clearly accept

this when they berate the blind man after he is cured. He says, "Well, do you want to be his disciples, too?" They say, "Are you telling *us,* you're saying that to *us,* you who have been steeped in sin since birth?" They are crediting his blindness with sin. Therefore, it is a reasonable question.

The Jews acknowledged that God would occasionally chastise those whom he loved for their own welfare, and that out of what seemed to be punishment, good would come. However, the rabbis taught that there was one punishment God would never inflict on anyone, even for their own welfare. It was a punishment so severe that it always had to be the fruit of sin. That was, not to be blind, but to be blind from birth. The reason the rabbis gave was that if you were blind from birth you were doomed to go through life without ever being able to read the scriptures. So, this was a punishment meted out only for sin, at least, according to popular conception.

Jesus says, however, "No, neither one of them sinned. This is not the result of sin. On the contrary, the purpose of this man being born blind is to let God's work show forth in him." By that, Jesus specifically meant "let my light shine forth. I am the Light of the World." Here, we can see, is an anticipation of Easter. In the context of the gospel, Jesus has yet to undergo his suffering, death, and resurrection. But he is going to do this very soon, and is actually going to demonstrate that he is a light that even the darkness of death cannot annihilate. As you know, we express this symbolically—liturgically—in the Easter fire, and by the Paschal candle, which we proclaim to be the Light of Christ, the Light of the World.

The Pharisees argued that the blind man's cure actually could not be from God because when Jesus mixed his spittle with mud, and put the paste on the blind man's eyes, he violated the Sabbath. There were, if I recall correctly, thirty-six kinds of work that would violate the Sabbath commandment to keep the Lord's day. This, apparently, was one of them. The purpose of the rules to keep the Sabbath holy was to give glory to God. However, some of these rules were taken to ridiculous extremes, and this was a case in point.

Jesus claims the same purpose for making the mud. The Pharisees say, "You made mud, you worked, and therefore you took glory away from God." Jesus says, "No, I did it to let God's glory shine forth. I did it precisely for the purpose that the Sabbath is kept holy." The man who was born blind has a very special role in all of this, even though it is somewhat passive. He is soon to make it very active when the Pharisees accuse him. "Since you're the one this was done to," they ask him, "it was your eyes he opened, what do you have to say?" Boldly the man responds, "He is a prophet. He is one who speaks for God."

At this point, we are beginning to deal with the real healing that took place, the real sight and the real insight that Jesus gave to this man. As we listen to this story, Jesus and the Pharisees talk about sight and blindness and go back and forth in what might be termed a series of puns or certainly irony. Sometimes the sight is referred to as the

Light of Christ, which allows us to see. Sometimes sight is known as physical sight. It is the same thing with blindness: sometimes blindness is disbelief, other times it is ignorance, sometimes it is even sin. To go from blindness to sight is to go from disbelief to belief and faith. This healing is typical of the few healings that Jesus did in terms of eyesight. His primary purpose was not giving eyesight, although that is a component. The physical healing is very secondary to the symbolic meaning. If we look briefly at another incident where Jesus gave sight to the blind, the blind man in Jericho, we can see why.

You will recall that the blind man in Jericho (Luke 18:35) called out and Jesus came to him and asked, "What do you want?" and he said, "Lord, that I may see." Jesus said to him, "Your faith has healed you." Now, what is meant by "your faith"? What is meant is that even though that man was blind, he *saw* Jesus, he acknowledged who Jesus was. So he had sight, or insight. This is why Jesus says, "Well, OK, since you've already got sight, now be healed."

Thus, the man opens his eyes, and interestingly the first thing he sees, even physically, is Jesus.

Luke's Gospel tells us that the formerly blind man carried his faith to its logical conclusion, because we are immediately told that "he followed Jesus on the way," (Luke 18:43) and the way Jesus was on at that time was the road going to Jerusalem to be crucified and rise from the dead. This man, Bar Timaeus, who had formerly been blind, because he was now sighted and insighted and had faith, was able to follow, physically and spiritually. This is the same thing that happens with the man born blind. It is only the first step that we see when the blind man says to the Pharisees: "He is a prophet." The scene is very dramatic.

When we speak of a person leaving one church or joining another we say he was converted or he joined another church. This is what St. John wants to tell us—that this man was converted from Judaism to Christianity. But he does it very graphically, because he says: "They threw him out bodily." The point is that the blind man became a Christian with the help of those who booted him out of the synagogue.

An interesting thing happens here. We are told that Jesus sought the blind man out and asked him, "Do you believe in the Son of Man?" Jesus is saying, "I know I've given this man eyesight, physical eyesight, now I want to carry through this process, and I want to give him true sight. I want to become for him his Light, not the light of the sun but myself, the Light of the World." This is why Jesus said to him, "Do you believe in the Son of Man?" What Jesus is actually saying is, "Do you really see? Have you really received your sight like that man in Jericho? Do you believe in the Son of Man?" The man says, "Who is he, that I may believe in him?" Then, to verify the interpretation I am giving, Jesus says to the formerly blind man, "You have seen him. It is he who talks to you now." So he says, "I do believe, Lord," and he bows down to worship him.

The Light of the World

This is a wonderful story, with marvelous symbolism and great power. What we have to ask ourselves now is, "What does this mean for us? How do we bridge the gap between those people and that event, and us today in our lives?"

We have to recognize the two people who are involved: one is the man born blind—that is you and I. The other is Jesus. The gospel brings the reality of these two people to us in this passage. Jesus said, "I am the Light of the World." Yet, he cannot be the Light of the World unless that light comes and is available to each one of us. If there is light and no one to see it, there really is no light. Light depends on the ability of people or things to respond to it. So, if no one responds to it, there is no light. It is like the old philosophical question: If a tree falls over in the forest and there is no one around, is there any noise? Well, if the world is enlightened, and no one is enlightened by it, is there really any light of the world? The answer, of course, is no.

For Jesus to be the Light of the World depends on you and me. Jesus sought out the blind man and he does the same thing to us. He comes to each one of us, and is seen in the beautiful symbolism of the Holy Saturday Easter vigil. When the fire is lit, from that fire comes Jesus, the Light of the World. Then from that fire the priest takes a taper and lights the Paschal candle, which is the Light of Christ. However, the light does not end there; because the light from the Paschal candle is given to every single person who is present, so that the Light of Christ, the Light of the World, becomes our personal light.

Again, we have to take that symbolism and work it out in the activities of our daily life. We are called to see by the light that Jesus gives us. We are called to see by the Light that Jesus himself is—never to see or view ourselves or our individual world apart from the Person of Jesus, the reality that Jesus is. If Jesus is the Light of our World, he has to be or become the motivating force in every activity. When Jesus is not behind everything we do, it is being done at least in partial darkness. Jesus is the deciding factor when we hesitate to make a decision.

Jesus, to be the Light of the World, must be the viewpoint from which we look out upon our individual worlds. He must be our guide, teacher, and the ultimate goal of our daily lives, indeed of our entire existence. We must constantly ask ourselves, in the small as well as in the major decisions and choices of our lives, "What would Jesus do? What would Jesus have me do? How should I act right now to respond to my commitment to Jesus? How can his teachings, his example, and his personal presence in my life illuminate my path?" In this way, our blindness will give way to light, and our lives will shine forth the glory of God.

7

Believe in Him

WILLIAM MENINGER

The Eighth Day of the Celebration
of Easter Sunday

In the evening of that same day, the first day of the
week, the doors were closed in the room where the
disciples were, for fear of the authorities. Jesus came
and stood among them. He said to them, "Peace be
with you," and showed them his hands and his side.
The disciples were filled with joy when they saw
the Lord, and he said to them again, "Peace be with
you. As the Father sent me, so am I sending you."
And saying this he breathed on them and said,
"Receive the Holy Spirit. For those whose sins you
forgive, they are forgiven; for those whose sins you
retain, they are retained."

Thomas, called the Twin, who was one of the
Twelve, was not with them when Jesus came. When
the disciples said, "We have seen the Lord," he

answered, "Unless I see the holes that the nails made in his hands and can put my finger into the holes they made, and unless I can put my hand into his side, I refuse to believe."

Eight days later, the disciples were in the house again and Thomas was with them. The doors were closed, but Jesus came in and stood among them. "Peace be with you," he said. Then he spoke to Thomas, "Put your finger here; look here are my hands. Give me your hand; put it into my side. Doubt no longer, but believe." Thomas replied, "My Lord and my God!" Jesus said to him, "You believe because you can see me. Happy are those who have not seen and yet believe."

There were many other signs that Jesus worked and the disciples saw, but they are not recorded in this book. These are recorded so that you may believe that Jesus is the Christ, the Son of God, and that believing this you may have life through his name. (John 20:19–31)

There are certain things that happen in our lives that we remember, sometimes simply because they are associated with the bigger holidays, such as Christmas and Easter. There is a rather dismaying incident in my life that I always remember and think of at this time of year. It happened about twelve years ago in Aspen. I was doing some last minute shopping—it was Holy Saturday, the day before Easter—and, while I was waiting in line in a store, there were two young men talking. One was the cashier, or the proprietor, and the other was a friend of his who was in the shop to purchase something.

I patiently waited until they went through their friendly greeting and then the young man who was the purchaser turned to go. As he reached the door he stopped, and said to his friend, the proprietor, "Well, I hope you have a Happy Holiday, but of course it's not a biggie, is it?" And his friend responded, "No, not much of a holiday." Well, my balloon was deflated. I was absolutely crushed upon hearing the claim that Easter is not much of a holiday, that it is not a biggie.

As you know, Easter is the biggest holiday of the Church, her most important festival. Indeed, it is so important that it has an eight-day octave. Today is the eighth day of the celebration of Easter Sunday. But it is more important than that, because it actually has a fifty-two-week octave. Every Sunday is a celebration of Easter, every Sunday is intended precisely to be a celebration of the resurrection of Christ. Now if these two men said it was not a biggie and many others agree with them, then for them it wasn't. My thought was, "Well, for this to be a biggie then something has to happen to make it so." It cannot be something that has the hype and commercial aspects of Christmas, or have Christmas-type things artificially introduced into it. Something has to happen to individuals to make it a biggie.

This bothered me no end because I wasn't preaching on Easter. I was, like this year, preaching on the octave of

Easter, which is still part of the great Holy Day. I felt I had to do something, at least in my homily, to convince people that it was a biggie.

Universal Symbols

Of course the first thing I did not understand was that the people who came to listen to my homily did so because they knew that Easter was a biggie. I really did not have to convince them; but I didn't think of that. I felt I had a responsibility, through my own powers of persuasion, to convince people that this was the greatest festival of the year, and, really, the most important day of their lives. I felt tremendously insecure at my ability to do this—or my inability to do this—and then felt guilty for feeling inadequate. It has only been very recently, after more than a decade, that God has given me the grace to realize that I do not have to convince everyone of how big Easter is. Indeed, I cannot do it.

Let me digress just for a moment. When you came into the church this morning I am sure one of the first things you saw was the Paschal candle. It is a very impressive symbol, placed in the middle of the church, on a special stand, with a beautiful wreath of leaves ascending it. The candle itself is unusual in its size and its decorations. We know that this candle is a symbol of the risen Christ; but it is a great deal more than that. When we look closely at the candle, we notice that it has, in the middle, bands of blue above and below. The band of blue on the top is beset with stars, to symbolize the creation of the cosmos. That is the first reading we have in the Easter vigil, God creating the world and all that was involved in it. This is because Easter is a new kind of creation. The lower blue band has wavy lines and fishes in it, representing the ocean. The sea for the ancient people of Palestine represented chaos. It was a symbol of one of their gods who had fallen from the heavens. Nowadays, the water symbolizes not chaos but a restoration to the oneness and the fullness of God's creation through baptism established by the resurrection of Christ.

If we look in the middle between the bands we see a large red cross, a universal symbol of our redemption in Christ. The unusual thing about it is that it is not like the crucifix. It does not have a body or figure on it. Instead, it has five large grains of incense, placed there to glorify the five wounds of Christ, because by his wounds we are healed. If you notice above and below the cross there are the Greek letters, *alpha*, the first letter of the Greek alphabet, and *omega*, the last. This means that everything between A and Z is contained here.

All of these images are what we would call universal, general symbols, and they are extremely important. They have tremendous truths contained in them, which have been—for approximately two thousand years—symbols that we understand and use to teach. But there is also something else.

There are two words for time in ancient Greek: *chiros* and *chronos*. Chronos is, as you might imagine, chronological time, the passage of minutes and hours. When we speak of time in the sense of chiros, however, we are speaking of another kind of time entirely. For example, we are thinking of chiros time when we say things like "these are times that try men's souls," or "it was the best of times and the worst of times." Chiros time is the time that belongs to mythology, the time that is universal, that has nothing to do with the passage of minutes. All of these symbols, the water and sky, the alpha and omega, the cross and the wounds, all belong to chiros, to the universal symbolism of time.

There is one thing, however, that is quite different on that candle. It is startlingly different because it does not belong to chiros, but rather to chronos, to time that is numbered. That is the date of the year. It is startling in its contrast actually. That date will never again be put on a Paschal candle. Next year the date will be different, just as last year the date was different. The point of using the year is to bring the meaning of these universal symbols—order and peace and light—home to us. We need to do so because we are not generic, mythological symbols. We are concrete, named people. Indeed, instead of the year, were it feasible, we could have somebody write on that candle the names of everybody who is here today. That is what the year's name means. It is a concretization, an application of all of the symbolism that the Paschal candle means. This involves us.

The Biggie in My Life

Those young men in Aspen did not understand how these symbols of Easter had anything to do with them. The challenge for all of us is to get from the general symbols of

Easter and the resurrection of Jesus into something concrete and relevant to our everyday lives.

When Jesus appeared on Easter Sunday after his death as the risen Lord, you will recall that he first appeared to Mary Magdalene. She thought he was the gardener, she did not know who he was. It was only when he spoke her name and said "Mary" that she did. Once Jesus had had that intimate, personal contact with Mary, she recognized the Lord. She ran and told the disciples, but they did not believe her. They probably assumed that she was just being a hysterical woman. Then, you will remember, the evening of Easter Sunday, Cleopas and the other disciple were walking to Emmaus (Luke 24) and Jesus joined them. They did not know who he was. They recognized him, however, when he celebrated the Eucharist with them at their home in Emmaus, and knew him in the breaking of the bread. Again, they did not believe until that personal sharing took place; and who is more personal than a companion, one who eats bread with you? Finally, there is the scene where Jesus appeared to the eleven and Thomas was not there and didn't believe. Thomas only believed when Jesus appeared to him and personally invited him to believe. Therefore, you can see that, even though the word that Jesus had risen had been announced by Mary, the disciples, Thomas, and the two disciples who had heard about it did not believe. It was only when Jesus actually came to them with personal, intimate contact that they really believed. Only those to whom Jesus personally presents himself believe.

In St. John's Gospel, Jesus says, "You believe because you can see me. Happy are those who have not seen, and yet believe." I have a slight problem with this statement because I think it is often misunderstood. My problem is that it suggests that I should be credulous, and accept everything that comes along. But I am not happy, because I have not seen him, and I would be a lot happier if I could have seen him. I, like Thomas, would like to touch his wounds, and verify the reality of them. Therefore, what are we to make of the statement, "happy are those who have not seen, and yet believe"?

Jesus is not talking about those who have not had personal contact with the risen Christ. That is not what he means at all, for there is a value and necessity in having the risen Christ brought to us and preached to us. Indeed, he told the disciples, "Go and do this throughout the world." But the mere knowledge of Jesus having risen is not in itself going to make people believe in the risen Christ, as we can see by the examples above. Thomas only comes to believe by being there with the other eleven; Jesus once again comes the week after his resurrection. It is the same with the disciples on the road to Emmaus. They are talking about the things that have happened, and wishing they were true, but they do not believe them. In a sense, they are still hanging on like the disciples who did not believe Mary Magdalene. They still stayed around. They were gathered together, waiting to see what would happen.

That is why we need our gathering on Sunday, the preaching, the communication, and the witness and the faith of others. We need the word of the scriptures to tell us that Jesus has risen from the dead. But we need something more. On the Saturday night or Sunday morning of Easter, when we have the Easter Vigil and the celebrant lights the Easter candle, it is the symbol of the resurrection of Christ. This is the mythological and general symbolic statement. But something wonderful happens. All the rest of us are, as it were, hanging around, candles in our hands. Then the priest takes the light from the Paschal candle and passes that light to each one of us. And there we have that personal contact. We have our own light of Christ. Jesus somehow touches us.

This is exactly what has to happen in order for us not only to see but to believe. It begins through this gospel, through the witness of the living Church. As St. John says, "These [signs] are recorded so that you may believe that Jesus is the Christ, the Son of God." Thus, it is through others that we come to believe, and grow to an even deeper belief.

I will never forget an incident, more than thirty years ago, when I was a retreat master at our mother house in Massachusetts. I had just given an Easter conference to a group of people who were in fact Baptists. Their minister was with them. After the conference, I went into the retreat master's office and was sitting there waiting for somebody to come in. The minister came and stood at the door and held out his arms. He looked me in the eyes and said, "Jesus is Lord, isn't it wonderful?!"

My understanding that Jesus is Lord has been enhanced ever since that moment, simply by that statement. The minister brought the presence of Jesus as Lord to me in a powerful way. In this way, I believed, even though I did not see. But that experience came ultimately not through this wonderful minister but through Jesus, who used the minister to bring himself to me. In this way, we are not cheated. We hear the Word, we see the signs that are given to us, and we see the faith of others. But, ultimately, Easter has meaning to us on a one-to-one basis because, as St. John says, by "believing this, you may have life through his name."

"In his name" means in the power of Jesus. This is how we believe and have life. Jesus presents himself to us personally and we accept that presence, that risen Christ. It is real and has meaning in our lives. Jesus gives us new life. When we say "life in his name" he personally touches us. And more than that, St. John brings out in the gospel passage that it is God the Trinity—Father, Son, and Holy Spirit—that is involved in this personal touching. You will recall when Jesus first comes he says, "Peace be with you. As the Father sent me..." He brings in the Father and then immediately adds, "Receive the Holy Spirit." When St. John touches his wounds, he says, "My Lord and my God," acknowledging Jesus as God. In this way, we have the power of God the Father, Son, and Holy Spirit bringing us to Christ. So, Christ personally touches us, if we are open through the Word, the Church, and other people who have faith. He strengthens us in our wavering doubts and insecurities, as he did Mary Magdalene, the disciples at

Emmaus, the eleven in the upper room, and the disciple Thomas. He touches us and, believing, we have life in his name.

What Is Important

Thomas Keating

The Seventh Sunday after Easter

Jesus raised his eyes to heaven and prayed, saying: "Holy Father, keep those you have given me true to your name, so that they may be one like us. While I was with them, I kept those you had given me true to your name. I have watched over them and not one is lost except the one who chose to be lost, and this was to fulfill the scriptures. But now I am coming to you, and while still in the world I say these things in the world to share my joy with them to the full. I passed your word on to them, and the world hated them, because they belong to the world no more than I belong to the world. I am not asking you to remove them from the world, but to protect them from the Evil One. They do not belong to the world any more than I belong to the world. Consecrate them in the truth; your word is truth. As you sent me into the world, I have sent them into the world, and for their sake I consecrate myself so that they too may be consecrated in the truth. (John 17:1, 11–19)

It is difficult to say something of any significance in the face of the great mystery that the Church is celebrating during these days of Jesus' resurrection and ascension. I know you are all looking forward to Pentecost, the greatest feast of the year, which is next Sunday. It is as if the greatest movie of the year was to be shown next Sunday, and you said to the family, "We can't miss it," and you look forward to it all week. The principal feasts of the Church are somewhat like that, except that instead of taking place on a screen, the action takes place inside us and in the local community. Whatever thrill or excitement there is to some spectacular event, the feasts of the Church year, however modestly celebrated (as here at St. Benedict), are blockbusters. They are sublime moments of grace; and grace is the self-communication of God. Instead of looking at a screen, we are looking into the face of the Ultimate Reality—your source, the source of the cosmos. This is big stuff.

Given all this, the question naturally arises: What are we going to do all week? Obviously we will be thinking of this great event that is going to engulf the Church with an amazing outpouring of grace. Christ symbolized by the Paschal candle that was lighted on the Paschal Vigil has ascended into heaven. On this day, in most parts of the world, this extraordinarily meaningful symbol that stands so humbly in the chapel is proclaiming to us that human life has ascended into the glory of God and is permeated and penetrated, even in its most dusty corners, by this glory.

As the Church Fathers tell us, human nature has ascended in Christ and is now, by faith, participating in the transforming grace poured into us by the grace of Christ's resurrection and ascension. On the feast of Pentecost, human nature will be crowned with the energy of divine love itself.

So, how can we think of anything else this week? Everything else seems nothing compared to this. This is why this period between the Ascension and Pentecost is a reliving of the original retreat that Jesus instituted when he told the disciples to wait for the Holy Spirit to come upon them in Jerusalem. Then the apostles will be able to go out and preach the Gospel because they will be the living Gospel. In their inmost being they will radiate the divine energy that is symbolized by the tongues of flame descending upon them.

This is the week when we prepare for the inconceivable—the descent upon us of the grace that descended as living tongues of flame upon the disciples in the upper room.

To be fully human is to be divine, because that is the way humanity is intended to be, and this is now about to happen. The key to being a Christian is to know Christ with the whole of our being. Such is the work of reading the scriptures prayerfully and being with people who know

Christ. They are passing on the living tradition of the Gospel in our time.

Intuitions

But to know Christ with the whole of our being requires a further step. The intuitive part of our human nature doesn't become active until we are about fifteen or sixteen. Up until then we are taking in all kinds of sense impressions that are preparing us to think and to be reasonably logical. But once the brain has reached a certain level of maturity, our intuitive sense begins to emerge. For many young people, the intuitive sense is retarded because they are preoccupied with their social lives, what their future professions will be, and other things that concern them in our culture.

The big question that lies at the depth of young people's hearts is: What is the meaning of life? Perhaps we don't give teenagers enough chance or a place that is suitable for them to ask that question in all sincerity. It's the biggest question a teenager can ask, and it is sometimes buried under all kinds of trivial concerns. The transcendent potential of adolescents begins to receive intuitions that come from the Holy Spirit. These insights would enable them to perceive the divine action and love working through the details of everyday life.

Finally, it is not enough to know Christ with the whole of *our* being. It is a great start, even if you only get started at seventy. But why not start sooner? Dare I suggest it— *now?* That is the meaning of the liturgical feast—*now* is the time of salvation, *now* is the time to open to the divine largesse.

What glorifies God is to communicate the absolute maximum of the divine light and love that we can possibly receive. That is why we must know Christ, not just with the whole of our being, but with the whole of *his* being: that is, to know him in his passion, to assimilate his teaching, and to try to imitate his moral integrity. This is to know Christ as a human being. But we must also know him in his divinity, as the Divine Person of the Word, as that infinite relationship in which the Father knows Himself in the Son, and in that infinite gift to humanity in which the Word of God became a human being.

Christ ascended beyond the clouds, not into a geographical location but into the heart of all creation, where he dwells as invincible light and as the Life of all that has life. How can we say "no" to God, to Light, to infinite Love? Yet this is the human condition; for it is easier to say "no" or "maybe tomorrow" than to say "yes," right now.

Let us surrender to the infinite Goodness that is approaching us. The awareness of God's attraction is like a black hole that irresistibly draws everything, including light, into its center. Once the divine attraction is released within us, there is no way of escaping its power. One's movement toward the center accelerates. Christ is a transforming, enormously attractive force drawing us into the Trinity and transforming us into the ultimate meaning of life, which is unconditional love.

9

Holy Trinity

THOMAS KEATING

The Feast of the Holy Trinity

Eleven disciples set out for Galilee, to the mountain where Jesus had arranged to meet them. When they saw him they fell down before him, though some hesitated. Jesus came up and spoke to them. He said, "All authority in heaven and on earth has been given to me. Go, therefore, make disciples of all nations; baptize them in the name of the Father, and of the Son, and of the Holy Spirit, and teach them to observe all the commands I gave you, and know that I am with you always, yes, to the end of time." (Matthew 28:16–20)

Today is the Feast of the Most Holy Trinity—the deepest of all the Christian mysteries and source of all the others. Mystery is something we can only know through faith. It transcends any concept that we can form of it.

I once heard a story about a storefront hospitality facility in Minneapolis that served as a coffee shop for the homeless and provided a staff to converse with them. One of the staff members noticed a homeless man who impressed him as very spiritual. In one of their conversations, he said, "I think you would like to read this spiritual book," and he handed him one by Thomas Merton, one of the great spiritual writers of this century. "I don't really want to read it," the man replied. But the staff member forced it on him, so the man finally took the book and was gone for a couple of days. Eventually, he showed up with the book and handed it back to the staff person, saying, "I really can't read this. Anyone who really knows God keeps his mouth shut."

Perhaps I could end the homily at this point, but I am reminded of Jesus' exhortation, "Preach the Good News to everybody and make disciples of all nations" (Matthew 28:19). Now, perhaps you can do this just by being silent. This is what hermits do, and to some extent monks of all traditions, by withdrawing from the world, keeping their mouths more or less shut, and hoping to transmit from their inner being the experience of Christ.

In any case, I will take a chance and say a few words, and hope not to be overwhelmed by the majesty of this great mystery. What can one say about it? One can only point to it, stumble, or stammer. But something apparently has to be said, and the liturgy is supposed to be such a time. So here we go, launching into the unspeakable, the incredible, the marvelous mystery that is beyond all words, thoughts, and experience.

You will remember that on the Feast of the Ascension two weeks ago the Lord Jesus ascended from his disciples into the heart of all creation, completing the resurrection process. And then on Pentecost, he bestowed upon them the riches of the Holy Spirit, which are his to give as the Eternal Word of God. As Paul says: "God has sent the Spirit of his Son into our hearts crying aloud 'Abba'—Father!" (Galatians 4:6). We might humbly ask the Spirit: "Who is 'Abba' to whom we cry out as a result of the infusion of your grace?"

"Abba" is a very intimate word. Apparently, it expressed Christ's consciousness of the Ultimate Mystery, as a paternal/maternal, loving, intimate, and tender presence—all the things that might be summed up when one says "Poppa" to a very dear earthly father.

Nicholas of Cusa (1400–1464) at the end of his life—at the summit of his own contemplation—calls God "to be able itself" *(posse ipsum* in Latin). To translate this phrase as "potentiality" is to fossilize the idea, whereas *posse* is a verb and suggests that the Father is infinite silence or emptiness that is not just a void, but eternally on the verge, so to speak, of coming to divine consciousness. The latter is expressed in an interior word, which the scripture calls the Son of God, the *Logos,* "the Word that enlightens everyone coming into the world" (the Prologue of St. John's Gospel).

When the Father expresses Himself, He gives Himself completely to the Son, the Eternal Word. The Father knows

Himself only in the Son, and the Son in turn knows himself only in the Father. When these two Persons, or infinite relationships, confront each other in the bosom of the Trinity, there rises up from their common heart a sigh of love that is not an aspiration to happiness, but the fulfillment of everlasting joy, an immense and total outpouring of one into the other in such a way that both are identified with the divine essence or godhead. In the Trinity there is no possessiveness, no self in any sense that we understand the term. There is simply the consciousness of infinite love.

The Inner Life of God
This inner life of God, summed up in the Person of unconditional love, is the Spirit that is given to us at Pentecost. Today, and hopefully over the course of the week, we will become conscious within ourselves of who the Trinity of persons are, and to *realize* that this infinite love of God is being transmitted to us. We need to grasp that this love has not only embraced us, but has become the very center of our inmost being, our true self.

It is as if in saying *Trinitas* we know there isn't anything else, so to speak. "God is all in all" (I Corinthians 15:28). Everything is contained in this mystery, and out of this mystery is meant to come all our activity—our thoughts, actions, and words. "Spirit" means "breath." Not only does breath sustain life, but (in an image that is particularly engaging) the Spirit is the breath that sustains speech. This Spirit also sustains weeping and laughter and song.

What is Spirit in the Trinity? It is the sigh of infinite love, one not of longing but of infinite satisfaction and fulfillment. The "Allelujah" of Eastertime tries to capture it. Within us, the Spirit is the source of all happiness, truth, and love arising not as our own, but as something in which we participate in the degree to which our own self-interests diminish and we accept this Spirit of God as our true and deepest self. We might say, therefore, that Lent is the Spirit within us crying out with longing for the happiness and truth for which we are designed and created. The mystery of Easter expresses the realization of the risen Christ recognizing himself in us, as if so say, "Hello, I've been here all the time. Where have you been?" We have been alienated and separated from our true self, and the Easter grace tears apart the veil of human effort to avoid God born out of fear. In the Pentecostal feast that we celebrated last week, Jesus, having entered into the fullness of the resurrection, breathes the Spirit not only upon his disciples but into you and me.

Here is where the amazing image of certain Church Fathers awakens in us an invincible hope. They describe the Spirit as "the most sweet kiss" of the Father and the Son. In a "most sweet kiss," lovers try to pour their whole being into each other, as the sign of immense love and total surrender to each other.

The sigh of love that awakens in us is the fullness of the Pentecostal grace in which—having longed for God and tasted the first fruits of inner resurrection—we fall silent, because, at this feast, there is nothing more for which to yearn or hope. God has become present not just in His oneness, with which He relates to all creation, but present in His most intimate and secret nature, hidden from all creation. That is why we call it a mystery, a mystery revealed through Jesus as the divine-human person and bestowed upon us in its fullness through Baptism, Confirmation, the Eucharist, and contemplative prayer.

What we are celebrating today, therefore, are not words or feelings, but the invincible faith that God dwells within us as infinite love—loving himself in us, and relating to himself in us, and within us relating to the mystery of unconditional love. This is the rest to which contemplation leads—a rest that is not inertia, but the fulfillment of every holy desire. Out of this union comes the need to do what God does, which is to serve all of creation according to our capacity or in the degree that we feel the Spirit is calling us. We do this by word and example, filled with the mystery of unconditional love, which, on this day, we are invited to experience.

10

The Body of Christ

Thomas Keating

The Feast of the Body and Blood of Christ (Corpus Christi)

Jesus said, "I am the living bread that came down out of heaven; if anyone eats of this bread, he will live forever; and the bread also which I will give for the life of the world is my flesh." Then the Jews began to argue with one another, saying, "How can this man give us his flesh to eat?" So Jesus said to them, "Truly, truly, I say to you, unless you eat the flesh of the Son of Man and drink his blood, you have no life in yourselves. He who eats my flesh and drinks my blood has eternal life, and I will raise him up on the last day. For my flesh is true food, and my blood is true drink. He who eats my flesh and drinks my blood abides in me, and I in him. As the living Father sent me, and I live because of the Father, so he who eats me, he also will live because of me. This is the bread which came down out of heaven; not as the fathers ate and died; he who eats this bread will live forever." (John 6:51–58)

The Church is still unpacking the riches of Easter, the Ascension, and Pentecost. The Ascension is when Jesus disappeared beyond the clouds—not into a geographical location, but into the heart of all creation. God then sent into our hearts his own Spirit so that we might awaken to the presence of Christ, in, through, and beyond everything that exists. Therefore, at Pentecost, we are told that "God has sent the spirit of his Son into our hearts crying aloud 'Abba'—Father" (Galatians 4:6).

There is a certain exaltation in the awareness that the Father, the source of all that is, is the source of our existence at every level but is also a living and personal relationship. At the Feast of the Holy Trinity, which is the Sunday immediately preceding the Feast of the Body and Blood of Christ, we celebrate the awakening in us of what the love of God is, which is the meaning of the Feast of Pentecost. The Spirit who has been given to us in the Pentecostal grace pours the love of God into our hearts. This experience is a further development of the grace of Easter and the Ascension. We can become aware of the treasures of grace contained in those feasts if we understand their significance for ourselves and for the whole world.

In the context of this unpacking process we come on this feast day to another momentous event of grace. The body and blood of Christ in the Eucharist is the structural means by which we increase the awakening that took place at Pentecost and the Feast of the Holy Trinity. These feasts tell us who we really are. They relate us to the Ultimate Reality. They plunge all our faculties into the world of grace, the bottom line of which is the Trinitarian life itself—the movement within the Ultimate Reality of infinite life and love.

To grasp the significance of this feast, I will do a little more unpacking and, more specifically, explore what happens in the celebration and reception of the Eucharist. We have a guide to this from the Second Vatican Council in its document *The Constitution on the Liturgy*. The Bishops of the Council identified four presences of Christ in the Eucharist. Each presence is a boundless treasure, so that even if you only hear the first one, you are in good shape for the week.

The Five Presences

Before we do anything in the service, before we even bless ourselves as we come into church, Christ is present by virtue of our *intention* to join the worshipping community. In other words, the grace of the Ascension means that Christ is abiding not only in the bosom of the Father, but in the bosom of the Church expressed in the local community. Since the Church is us, Christ is abiding in *our* inmost being. We need to get acquainted with this presence. Actually, Christ is our deepest self, our true self. It is up to us to awaken to the immensity and incredible significance of this presence. So, just by being in church or by our intention as a community, we make Christ present.

The second presence of Christ in the Eucharist occurs when the Gospel is proclaimed. This is not just a reading, not just a talk show. The presence of Christ is hidden in the words that you hear. It is in the silence between the syllables. It supports what you hear, and it communicates the presence of Christ to those who are prepared to listen. The better you are prepared through deepening your listening skills the more you are in touch with the deeper presences of Christ that are available to us. The Eucharist is the primary structure for increasing that awareness.

Some of the saints have been changed while listening to the gospels proclaimed during the liturgy. Actually, the gospels are read every day, and address the particular problems or joys we face each day. The gospels mirror the graces that we are receiving in our daily lives. They are parables of our personal history as it is shaped and influenced by grace. Sometimes the gospels console us; at other times they challenge us deeply. For instance, suppose you heard Christ speaking the words, "If you want to be perfect, go and sell your possessions and give the proceeds to the poor. Then come back and be my follower"(Matthew 19:21). Those words may not be directed to everyone. I imagine that most members of religious orders as well as many others have heard those words directed to them.

Saint Anthony the Great of Egypt heard them and immediately went out and sold everything he had. But he kept a little bit for his younger sister whom he was looking after following their parents' untimely death. When Anthony went back to church a few days later God directed these words of the gospel to him, "What are you worrying about the future for?" Immediately, Anthony went out, sold the rest of his material possessions, and placed his sister in a convent with some reliable nuns to bring her up. We would naturally think it was wise of him to keep a little money aside to educate his sister and to take proper care of her. But God's ideas are not quite ours, and he wanted the surrender of everything from this man. Similarly, St. Francis of Assisi's conversion is based on this text. He heard not just the spoken words of the text at the liturgy but the voice of Christ challenging him at a point in his spiritual journey when he had to make a life-changing decision.

The third presence of Christ in the Eucharist, after we have entered the church to pray and listened to the scripture readings, is the actual physical presence of Christ's glorified body that becomes present on the altar through the Eucharistic prayer. This is the work of the Spirit, who has glorified Christ's body by devouring it in the flames of infinite love until it has been totally transformed into a purely spiritual presence. This brings Christ close to us—closer than he was to his disciples on the roads of Jerusalem or in Galilee.

Finally, this physical presence that is given to the whole community to bind the assembly into one, is offered to each member of the community in holy communion. Christ unites each of us to himself, not only through the community as a whole, but one by one, as individuals. This fourth presence crowns the Eucharistic celebration.

There is, however, a fifth presence. It is not mentioned in *The Constitution on the Liturgy*, but is presupposed. It is that the physical presence of us communicating Christ's body and blood—the physical union with Christ's body— that is the real sacrament of our being flooded and united to the divinity of the Word, the source of Christ's presence. As we eat the bread and drink the wine, believing that it is the body and blood of Christ, we are nourished by the Eternal Word of God that floods our spirits and feeds our souls with the torrents of divine love that flow from the sacred humanity of Christ into each of us.

In this way, the gift of Christ begins to be a part of our ordinary consciousness. One Eucharist could make that transformation permanent. In any case, as we receive this sacrament again and again, the body and blood of Christ transforms us into the dispositions of Christ, manifested by the fruits of the Spirit and the Beatitudes. Our whole value system is changed into the value system or mind of Christ. This fifth presence makes us aware of the divine presence that has been with us from the time of our creation, and supernaturally from the time of our baptism or our conscious desire for God. This presence expresses itself in the conviction that the Word of God is living in us and assimilating us to Himself. Now our words and deeds are beginning to be the words of God and the signs of God's presence.

The Father is infinite potentiality, speaking the Word in an eternal silence, and this Word in turn utters us and all of creation, and brings us to the fullness of the knowledge of the Father's love. Through this redeeming process, we return to the source of nature and of grace, and become one with God, not numerically of course, but manifesting God's goodness in our smallest as well as our most significant actions.

This is the awakening that is celebrated at Easter and more fully at the Ascension. The Eucharist is the structure that enables that awakening to continue and to become more pervasive. Eventually, that transformation invades each of our faculties until the very susbstance of our being is changed. Then we know the love of God that has been poured into our hearts by the Spirit who is given to us.

The Eucharist—as one of the prayers of the seventh Sunday after Easter says—is the sacrament of forgiveness. When we humbly approach the Eucharist with faith in the risen Christ and sorrow for our sins, when we depart, sin has vanished. It has vanished because the Eucharist is its annihilation.

Come and See
—Lectio Divina

JOSEPH BOYLE

The Second Sunday of Ordinary Time

As John was standing with two of his disciples, Jesus passed, and John stared hard at him and said, "Look, there is the Lamb of God." Hearing this, the two disciples followed Jesus. Jesus turned round, saw them following, and said, "What do you want?" They answered, "Rabbi"—which means Teacher— "where do you live?" "Come and see," he replied. So they went and saw where he lived and stayed with him the rest of that day. It was about the tenth hour.

One of these two who became followers of Jesus after hearing what John had said was Andrew, the brother of Simon Peter. Early next morning, Andrew met his brother and said to him, "We have found the Messiah"—which means the Christ. And he took Simon to Jesus. Jesus looked hard at him and said, "You are Simon, son of John; you are to be called Cephas"—meaning Rock. (John 1:35–42)

Last Sunday, we celebrated the Baptism of the Lord, and with that celebration we brought to completion the whole Christmas cycle of the liturgical year—a cycle that had begun with Advent and had the twin peaks of Christmas and Epiphany. We were looking at the mystery of Christ manifesting right in our midst, and with this week we now begin the ordinary time of the year.

The focus shifts a little, Of course, Christ is still the center of that focus, but now in the light of that focus we seem to be getting right into the picture. At this time, a number of questions emerge: We know that Christ has come, but what does that mean for us? What are we going to do about it? Where are we with regard to the question of discipleship?

The readings this morning are very beautiful, especially the first and the third, touching on our experience of discipleship. In the first reading we saw little Samuel in the temple being called by God and not knowing what to do, and finally being given this prayer that when he hears God calling he should say, "Speak Lord, your servant is listening," It is a great prayer for all of us. "Speak Lord, your servant is listening" (I Samuel 3:1–14).

The gospel reading we had today, from the Gospel of John, is also incredibly rich with the whole topic of discipleship. What I would like to do is to spend my time with you exploring this gospel, what it means for us, what it says about life, and what it can teach us. I want to read it much as we do *lectio divina* (spiritual reading). What *lectio divina* entails is taking a brief phrase and letting it reverberate inside us, touching off different levels of meaning. In particular, I want to focus on just three lines, the dialogue between Jesus and those two disciples who followed him, where Jesus asks, "What is it that you are seeking?" The disciples respond, "Teacher, where do you live?" and Jesus replies, "Come and see."

In these three lines there is a great wealth. It is not as if I want to read ideas into those sentences that are not there. On one level, we can look at the sentences and say, "That is a pretty simple dialogue. Two guys are following Jesus, and he turns around and says: 'What are you looking for?' and they say 'Well, where do you live?' and he says 'Come and see.' " But I can assure you that if that was all the dialogue was about John would not have put it in the gospel. All of our gospels have levels of meaning, and in John especially—John who is called the Theologian—there are many levels of meaning. So there is that simple discourse which propels the story, and there is also within that brief discourse a bringing together of a theology of discipleship, and this is in the first chapter of John's Gospel. John brings together things which took a very long time for the disciples to get, and he puts them in that first chapter, compressing them and making them very simple. He is giving us a picture of this discipleship. This is the theme I want to discuss.

Watching the Disciples

Although it is the disciples whom we are following and watching, at the same time we are also aware that it is really we who are being talked about in this passage. We are not solely interested in the passage from a historical perspective as something that happened two thousand years ago. What we are searching for are the answers to the questions: Where am I in this story? How is this affecting me? What is my encounter with Christ? What is Christ saying to me? And then, what is my response to him? These are the other issues we are watching. Therefore, we have the story of the disciples and yet we are the reality; we are looking at a mirror. Does what I see there correspond to my experience? Does it fit? Does it have something to teach me?

Let us get to the context. The two disciples, Andrew and John, were followers of John the Baptist, so they were already seekers on the spiritual path. They have been listening to what John the Baptist has to say. Then, when John sees Jesus go by one morning, John says, "Behold, the Lamb of God." Andrew and John then start following Jesus. Jesus sees them and turns around and asks them what they want.

Here we encounter a new level of meaning. What Jesus is saying is deeper than it would appear. He is asking, "What do you really want? What are you looking for? What are you seeking? What is your goal in life? What is it that gives meaning to your life, that gives meaning to everything else that you do—what is the centerpiece? What is your focus?

What is your heart's desire?" All of this is contained in that one question of Jesus, "What do you want?"

If I were smart, I would probably stop right there with that question of Jesus, and ask you to think about it and take it to heart. We have all come here this morning to mass, some from far away, some of us from just down the hall in this very building. But we have gathered here at this mass, and my guess is that if I could read the minds of people, there would be lots questions rattling around in our minds. "What kind of day is this going to be? What am I going to do later on? Shall I go skiing today or not? I wonder who is going to be at this liturgy? I wonder how long the sermon is going to be?"

On and on our minds run. We do not always notice how much they do run on and on.

However, if we take the time for meditation and try to sit quietly and empty our minds we get to see all the scenarios and stories that keep running through them. These scenarios go on throughout the day, no matter what we are doing. They distract us and pull us here and there. Then, all of a sudden, there is this word of Jesus, "What are you seeking?" And it focuses us, brings our scattered energies together. We are forced to ask ourselves, "Yeah, what *is* it that I'm seeking? What *is* my heart's desire? What *is* it that's most important in my life and gives meaning to the rest of my life?" These questions are worth pondering. They really are critical questions in life. So, like I say, if I were smart I would stop and just let you think about them.

Clearly, however, I am not that smart, so I want to go on and look at how the disciples respond to this question, and Jesus' invitation after that.

When the disciples are asked by Jesus what they are seeking, they do not give him a theoretical answer. They do not say, "Well, here's my project in life and these are the pieces of it and how I see it unfolding." Instead, they come back with another question, "Master, Teacher, where do you live?" In other words, the disciples are going to respond to the question not at the level of ideas but at the level of life. They push the question back to Jesus, back into the encounter, so that the encounter can grow and deepen. What they are saying, in effect is, "Tell us, Jesus, where *you* live, what you are about." The ball is back in Christ's court.

The scholars tell us that the word we translate as "live" is *menein* in Greek. It is a word used later in the gospel in a passage such as, "The Father and I will come and live, *abide* in you" (John 15:9). So the living we are talking about in asking the question "Where do you live?" is a very deep reality. It refers to the abiding presence of God in Christ and in us. What we are talking about is very substantial. The word "live" also carries a meaning, as if the disciples were saying to Christ, "What is your foundation? Where do you draw life from? What nourishes you? What gives meaning to *your* life?"

What the disciples are asking from their teacher are not ideas, but where *he* gets his life from, what his life is like, what the energy source that flows in him is. That is what they want to touch. And again, what is Christ's answer? He is not going to spell out a theory; he is not going to give them some ideas they can copy down in their notebook. His answer challenges them, "Come and see." What Christ means is that he doesn't want to tell them something they can just think about. He wants to give them something they have to come into and experience. "I want to give you a share of my life," Jesus is saying, "and you can come and share that life as I live it, as I experience it—then you'll know what my life is, where I live. So come and see." What Jesus wants is for the disciples to know that life from the inside—not just to have information, but to experience it from within, the way he lives from within. "Take it into your hearts," he is telling them, "and really live it as I live it."

Now, I am not trying to diminish the mind and intellect. I think it is important in life to have things in order and our goals worked out. However, in this exchange, Jesus is pushing us to a deeper level. "What is the life experience that's *under* all this thinking and organizing that we're doing?" Jesus is asking. "What is the core of our living?"

Dangerous Minds

There are some dangers when we start our minds working on things. One of those dangers is that we can be satisfied with thinking. We have a good theory; it pleases the mind. There is a certain satisfaction for us as intellectual beings to be able to say, "That looks good; it works out." This is fine. But if we stop there, we are not really engaged in living yet.

It is a component, and a helpful one. But it is still just a piece. So there can be a temptation to stop at that point. Christ, however, is pushing further. He is talking about what gives us life, about what gives us energy, what focuses our orientation.

It seems to me there is another danger, one that is quite similar but a step beyond thinking. We can hear someone give us a good program, we can listen to Christ, and we can try and put it into our lives and actions. But we never take it within so that it comes from inside ourselves. The program stays almost as something outside us. We see it out there; it looks good, and we try to make our actions conform to it.

Again, this is not a bad thing; it just isn't enough. What I see with that "Come and see," is a further invitation: "Come and get the spirit out of which I am living. Come deep into the world I want to open up to you. Come so that you see what I see, and love what I love." And all action flows from that. In this inner connectedness with Jesus we can begin to enter into Jesus' relationship with the Father, his trust that the Father was always caring for him, and enter into Jesus' love for his brothers and sisters, his compassion and his forgiveness. This was his life, his center, where he lived. This is what he is offering us, this inner world from which our actions flow.

When I was reflecting on this yesterday, the words of Paul came into my mind, "I live now, not I, but Christ lives in me" (Galatians 2:20). That is the reality, the shared life, and the discipleship. It is not just that our actions look like

Christ's actions, but the mind and the heart out of which the actions come reflect the mind and the heart of Christ. There is a deep oneness out of which the love flows. So, "Come and see."

How We Come and See

The question remains: How? John and Andrew were able to simply come and talk with Jesus, watch how he did things, and to some extent get his spirit. But we do not have that option, so we have to ask what it means for us to "Come and see." I believe that "Come and see" means somehow an inner opening in faith to Christ, an inner opening in faith that we put into action in different ways.

One way for Christians would be a reading of the scriptures, of the word of God, a reading that we take to heart. It would not be just a scholarly reading, which is important and helps us, but one that passes beyond the scholarly to the encounter with God *in lectio,* an inner quiet, an openness and receptivity so the word can get into us and change us deep down.

I also feel that "Come and see" is in our encounter in prayer, which flows straight from scripture reading. It is that quiet prayer when we put aside the thoughts of the day and of the things we need to do. It is when we put aside our many responsibilities which have to be worked out and just try to settle into the presence of God. We even need to put aside the different pious notions and preconceptions we have and just try, in our emptiness, to let God speak and be. It is not as if we normally will hear a word from God at those moments. Once in a while, it does happen. But that is not normally the way; most of the time we just sit there quietly.

What I am saying is that the quiet, receptive prayer, along with the reading, sets up a whole pattern of life for us. We carry that required surrender and receptivity, that openness to God and discipleship, into everything we do, into all encounters and relationships. We begin to hear God's word to us and his invitation. What we need flows out of that "Come and see."

Finally, I fear that the way I have described discipleship and centered on that phrase "Come and see," and talked about quiet, deep listening, suggests that discipleship appears as something passive, that it is a little withdrawn from life, perhaps even unproductive. If that is what you heard, then I have really failed to make my point, because discipleship is the exact opposite of passive, unproductive, and withdrawn.

Discipleship is ultimately very dynamic. I am focusing on the beginning of discipleship because that is the process I see at work in the reading. We go to Christ and touch the core of his life, so that our actions come out of that core. All the people whom I know to be really pursuing the path of listening deeply are people who are very dynamic. Let us return to the reading from Samuel, and the boy who says that prayer, "Speak, Lord, your servant is listening." As Samuel grew up, and I presume he kept that prayer and that attentiveness going, he became this incredibly dynamic figure in Israel speaking the word of God to the people, anointing kings and telling them what to do. In the gospels, what person in history do we know who is more dynamic than Jesus? Or John and Andrew, the disciples in this story? Andrew got his brother Peter and the rest of that crowd to become disciples and look at what they did!

Or, to turn to the present day, I think of the people I have known in the centering prayer movement. There is one fellow on the East Coast who, out of centering prayer, developed a desire to help the poor and the needy in the Caribbean, especially in Haiti. He started Food for the Poor, a group that has grown into a giant organization collecting food from places in the United States and sending it to starving people. On the West Coast there is something very similar. The program Share, which largely works in the inner cities, not only distributes food but creates community in the process. Share came from one person who, again, told me it came out of his practice of centering prayer.

So discipleship, when it is rooted in this deep listening, actually becomes something dynamic in our lives. What I see in this passage is that we are invited by this gospel into that core experience out of which the actions flow. We are invited into that deep relationship, a relationship even beyond words, out of which our lives flow. What I suggest is, during this week, that we take these three lines, any one of which can be a full meditation in itself, and play with them, let them resonate in our minds and hearts. See what pieces of you they hit and how they invite you into a space.

"What is it that you are seeking?"
"Teacher, where do you live?"
"Come and see."

12

Come and See
—Where Do We Live?

JOSEPH BOYLE

The Fifth Sunday of Ordinary Time

On leaving the synagogue, Jesus went with James and John straight to the house of Simon and Andrew. Now Simon's mother-in-law had gone to bed with a fever, and they told him about her straightaway. He went to her, took her by the hand, and helped her up. And the fever left her and she began to wait on them.

That evening, after sunset, they brought to him all who were sick and those who were possessed by devils. The whole town came crowding round the door, and he cured many who were suffering from diseases of one kind or another; he also cast out many devils, but he would not allow them to speak, because they knew who he was. In the morning, long before dawn, he got up and left the house and went off to a lonely place and prayed there. Simon and his companions set out in search of him, and when they found him they said, "Everybody is looking for you." He answered, "Let us go else-where, to the neighboring country towns, so that I can preach there too, because that is why I came." And he went all through Galilee, preaching in their synagogues and casting out devils. (Mark 1:29–39)

This morning's gospel reading gives us a picture of Jesus that provides, I believe, some very important lessons for you and me for our own daily lives. Some of you will recall that when the Christmas season ended some weeks ago and we started the ordinary time of the year, we saw a little shift in focus from being centered on Christ to the mystery of discipleship. We have seen what was happening with Christ; now we ask what shape that is going to take in our lives. What change is it going to make for us? How are we going to respond to Christ?

In the gospel reading that began the last chapter we saw the disciples Andrew and John follow Jesus, after John the Baptist had pointed him out as "the Lamb of God." Jesus saw them and he asked, "What are you seeking?" They responded, "Master, where do you live?" and Jesus replied, "Come and see." What I see in this chapter's gospel text is part of that invitation to come and see where and how Jesus lives. What is life like for him? What makes him tick? What are the values operative in him that manifest in his actions? What can we learn from them?

What I see in the gospel text is something of a tale of two loves. There is the love that Christ has for all of humanity. It is a love without any exclusions, a love that reaches out, cares, and is whatever it can be for anyone in need. It heals someone who is sick, teaches someone looking for wisdom, and pours itself out for others. Then there is that other love that was the prime love of his life. It lay underneath the first love, pushing itself up into the love for others. This was the love Jesus had for God, whom he called Father. It was *this* love that would drive him, tired as he was, to get up and go out to the mountain by himself and pray, and be alone in the presence of God. You see these two loves working in Jesus in this short gospel passage, and radiating a message to us. How do we work these two loves in our lives? How do they balance? How do they interact? It seems to me that if we are going to listen to the gospel and take it to heart, we have a few obstacles to overcome at first reading, so that we can see ourselves in that gospel.

Overcoming the Obstacles
The first obstacle is this: Jesus was evidently some kind of a miracle-worker, a real healer. So we see him not just helping people, but *curing* them. When they are sick, Jesus picks them up so that, for instance, the mother-in-law can get dinner. Jesus can make the blind see and the deaf hear and the lame walk again. Most of us don't have that ability! So we see a distance, between Jesus and ourselves.

However, this is not really an obstacle, because miracles are not what is important. What is important is the love that is moving Jesus to reach out—the caring, the opening of his heart to whoever had pain or need—is something we can reflect in our own lives. That is the message

Jesus gives to us again and again. In our lives, we are going to care for people, not by working miracles (we would if we could, but most of us can't), but in whatever way we can. We can work for healing in our different relationships, even in our jobs.

This message reaches deeply into our everyday lives. For it is not just the doctors, nurses, teachers, and counselors who can serve, but the bus driver who gets us from one place to another, the plumber who fixes our broken pipes, or the person who cooks our dinner, or all of us in the many other ways that we care for and serve each other. The service depends on its source. If our service is just a job, a way to get money, then, while meeting those needs is important, that service is limited. However, if there is also love at the center of our service, which is reaching out to others whom we are serving kindly and compassionately, then I see it as the same thing that Jesus is doing. That service is the love of one's neighbor manifesting itself, the love we are called to deep down. Therefore, I believe there is a parallel between Jesus' service and our own, even though Jesus' miracles at first may seem so different from what we can do. In the end, the miracle is a story of love, reaching out, caring, and doing what we can with the gifts we have.

There can be another aspect to it, at least in my imagination, where I find distance between Jesus and myself. It is when Jesus works out this balance of prayer, love of God and love of one's neighbor. Many of us these days are so busy, leading lives that are so hectic. We are doing three things at once, and, while we are doing those three things, we have someone on hold on the phone, there is a fax coming in, and e-mail is stacking up in the mailbox on our computer. We say to ourselves, "Life is so hard! We have got things to face that other people, certainly Jesus, didn't have to deal with."

If you are like me, you sometimes imagine Jesus strolling about the Holy Land with all the leisure of a modern day tourist, guidebook in one hand, looking up at the Mount of the Transfiguration and attending a few of the other gospel incidents as if he had all the time in the world to walk up and down the length of Palestine. However, when we look into the gospel text that begins this chapter, we see something different.

When Jesus comes home, the mother-in-law is sick. He performs the healing and has supper, and then all of the townsfolk begin to come to him, bringing people to be healed. "They crowded about," the text says, filled up the whole evening, so that when he got to bed he was dead tired. Then Jesus gets up in the middle of the night so he can go out and pray. Jesus doesn't have leisure time. And this happens to him over and over again; it isn't just one occasion.

In another passage later in the gospel, there is a scene where Jesus is teaching, and his mother and his brothers are outside trying to get at him because they think he is out of his mind. They think he hasn't even stopped to eat. What is he doing with all these people, performing all these miracles, doing all this teaching, they want to know, when all they want to see is that he gets a real meal? Jesus is facing demands from people on every side. He is teaching, and when there are no crowds he has disciples whom he is trying to teach and hand on his message to so they can carry it on.

With his disciples, you can see what he has to work with! Even in the gospel text in this chapter, the disciples do not get up to pray. They haven't got that part of the message yet. When they finally do find Jesus they say, "Lord, they're all looking for you. You've got to go back there." And Jesus says "No. I've got to go this way to other people who haven't heard my message." The disciples and Jesus are heading in opposite directions. Sometimes I get the feeling that Jesus' chore with the disciples is rather like a teacher trying to teach calculus to third-graders. We feel all of that frustration and drag that fills the off-hours when the disciples and Jesus are walking between scenes.

The Demands of Prayer

There is a scene toward the end of the rock musical *Jesus Christ Superstar,* by Andrew Lloyd-Webber and Tim Rice, where all the sick and the needy people, and those who want teaching, are reaching out for Jesus and calling to him. Jesus is being pulled this way and that, everybody wanting a piece of him. I don't know how inspired that musical was, but I think the scene really captured something of Christ's life as we see it in different areas of the gospel. All sorts of people wanted something from him. He didn't have a life of just simple holy leisure. He was pouring himself out, and had to make the time as you and I have to make the time, to pray, to pull aside, and to take quiet, personal time alone with God. As far as I can see, it was not all that different for Jesus.

There is another area where we might feel a difference between Jesus and us. This is in our prayers. When you and I set aside this quiet time and pray, sometimes there are very consoling moments and a sense of wide awakening. It feels so good to be connected to God like this. However, at other times, the experience is somewhat empty, perhaps even bleak or dry.

Even the saints, when they write about their prayer, tell us about periods and stretches of their lives when prayer was not very consoling and comforting; yet they persisted by virtue of a faith and perseverance and openness in that spirit of faith. This kind of persevering prayer is very important, maybe more important than consoling prayer. However, it is not an attractive force that can simply pull us from what we are doing because it is so consoling.

I think we imagine that Jesus as the Son of God could just walk aside and sit down and have a conversation with the Father. As Christians we believe that Jesus is the Eternal Word of God. So, Jesus is always with the Father. But, in his human nature, we have from the author of the Epistle to the Hebrews, he was like us in all things but sin and he experienced all of our limitations. So, when I imagine Jesus going off to pray, I don't imagine that it is all that different from the faith that we are called to—an openness, willingness, and intention to be in the presence of God. Jesus is receptive, open to hearing a word that may come months later or years later. But Jesus took that time and was receptive, just like you and I need to take that time and be receptive.

Finally, more and more people are recognizing that the pace of life we live today not only can wear us down and kill us, but it can make us counter-productive. We are so busy and yet we are not getting as much done as we feel we should. So we have management consultants telling people in business and throughout the company, "Take a break for meditation, take a break for yoga, tai chi out on the lawn," different things of that sort. We are finally recognizing a need for balance against this high-speed productivity. What I want to say is that, while this kind of activity is fine and worth doing, what I am talking about is something different. This is not something that rests our nervous system so we can become more productive in the next period. I am talking about an encounter with God.

Pulling aside to pray is not just a break from activity. It is a very genuine encounter, an opening, a personal relationship with God. It involves a love that is at the center, at the center of Jesus for sure, and at the center of our lives as well. This is what we nurture in that quiet time, however we work this balance in our lives. Therefore, what I suggest is that we have this gospel passage in front of us, as we play with it in our minds this week. Let us ask ourselves: "How does this relate to me? What is it saying? How do these two loves work in my life? How much of my activity really comes from a love inside me, or how much is something I just need to get done or I get fired? How much is manifesting out of a desire for service?" With that other love, the one that grounds the love of our neighbor, we should ask: "Do I take the time? Do I make the time to be alone with God, even if that encounter is quiet, empty, a waiting? Do I make the time so that my life really is flowing from that love? That love is grounding me?"

This is what I see when I look at Jesus. This is what I feel he is calling me to. Each of us had a different balance in our lives, a different set of gifts we bring to others, a different way of praying. Somehow we need to work with this balance so these two loves are what sit at the core of our being. It is what we are invited to be.

13

The Heart of Jesus

THEOPHANE BOYD

The Eighteenth Sunday of Ordinary Time

When once the crowd saw that neither Jesus nor his disciples were at the place where Jesus had eaten the bread, they too got into the boats and crossed to Capurnaum to look for Jesus. And when they found him on the other side they said to him, "Rabbi, when did you come here?" And Jesus answered, "I tell you more solemnly, you are not looking for me because you have seen the signs, but because you had all the bread you wanted to eat. Do not work for the food that cannot last, but work for food that endures to eternal life, the kind of food the Son of Man is offering you, for on him the Father, God Himself, has set his seal." And they said to him, "What must we do if we are to do the works that God wants?" And Jesus gave them this answer, "This is working for God. You must believe in the one He has sent." And so they said, "What sign will you give to show us that we should believe in you, what work will you do? Our fathers had manna to eat in the desert. The scripture says, 'He gave them bread from heaven to eat.'" And Jesus answered, "I tell you most solemnly, it was not Moses who gave you bread from heaven. It is My Father who gives you the bread from heaven, the true bread, for the bread of God is that which comes down from heaven and gives life to the world." "Sir," they said, "give us this bread always." And Jesus answered, "I am the bread of life. He who comes to me will never be hungry. He who believes in me will never thirst." (John 6:24–35)

This Sunday, last Sunday, and next Sunday feature the section of St. John's Gospel that is about the bread of life. It starts with Our Lord teaching the people at great length and then, when it's getting late, feeding them from five loaves and two fishes. The people are so taken with his teaching, and then with this multiplication of the loaves— feeding several thousand people—that they would like to make him king. Our Lord perceives that, and sends them away. He's not buying into that. He sends the apostles away, and goes up into the hills and spends the night in prayer. The next morning the people come back, and they want some more. They follow him, find him, and he says to them: "You're just following me because you got that bread to eat." In St. John's Gospel, we typically have to go back and forth between something understood first on one level, and then on a deeper, higher, level. The people are thinking about food to eat for their bodies, and Jesus is talking about the true bread, the real thing from God.

By way of comment on this I just have two questions. The first question pertains to these two levels. Nowadays there's a lot of interest in food and what we're eating. We are aware of additives, sugar, sodium, cholesterol, fat, and so on. The health food stores that are growing up all over reflect a preoccupation with food in the ordinary sense. But what about food in this other, higher sense? What nourishes you on a higher level? We look at the cows munching alfalfa and we know there's more to life than that. We also nourish our minds and spirits in some higher way. We read books, we watch television, we go to movies, we have conversations. This is all nutrition for our mind on some higher level. My question is: Where do you go for that higher food? Where do you go for nourishment on this other level?

If you think about this question, and, for instance, you typically watch television for hours and hours, you might realize, "My diet is a lot of junk food. Now, what do I do for something more substantial?" And people would have different answers for that. I've lived in the monastery long enough to know that the monastery is set up for that purpose, to present a higher food, regularly. Every day in the monastery there are readings from the Old Testament and the New Testament, and you chant some of them, and you ritualize—not just once a week, but every day, so you're getting nourishment all the time. Monks have a lot of leisure time other people don't have. We get up early in the morning, and we have a couple of hours of leisure time to nourish ourselves on that higher level through prayer, meditation, and private reading.

Yet, I can think of monks I've known who have not nourished themselves very well. Some, for instance, are into rational stuff. They may be scripture scholars, and yet it doesn't seem to get into their lives; it doesn't produce the charity or humility you might expect. Meanwhile, others may be pious but they haven't really developed their critical sense. But my question is not about other people; it's about us. It is embarrassing when I think about this higher level and ask of myself, "What do I feed my mind and my consciousness with? How much junk food, and how much substance?"

I hope it's clear that I want you to think about how you feed your mind, your consciousness, and your spirit. I know a lot of people feed their mind by coming to this monastery. The quiet, the atmosphere do things for them. But you need to think about this question for yourself. On the lower level I have this food for my body, physical life; and on this higher level, how do I nourish myself?

Now to the second question. Suppose in your parish you had a pretty good priest—he's gone through two six-year terms and has to move. So he moves, and a new priest comes, and (guess what?) the new priest is Jesus himself! Now, you don't know that. It's not advertised, but that's who it is. He looks like any other priest, but he's got the heart of Jesus. What would it be like if your pastor had the heart of Jesus and spoke and related to the people out of that? What would that do to the community? What would it do to the younger or the older people? Or, if you want to take it a little beyond that question, suppose Jesus came to the place where you work? Or if Jesus were the father of your children, what would that be like? What would that be like? That is my question.

There's a danger in questions like this. They are easy to apply to somebody else, so you start criticizing your pastor because he's not up to the level of Jesus. I hope that you don't do that, but make it a question about your heart. If you want to use the Magic Monastery, you go to the Magic Monastery, and when the old monk asks you what you'd like, you say, "I'd like to get the heart of Jesus." What if he reached out and took your heart right out of you, and he gave you the heart of Jesus? What would that be like? What difference would that make?

So, first, consider where you go for higher nutrition of your mind, spirit, and consciousness. Second, think about Jesus and his heart and how he is the bread himself—not simply what he says, but he himself, as we have here in the gospel: "I am the bread of life. He who comes to me will never be hungry. He who believes in me will never thirst." Check inside yourself to look for that hunger. We all have hunger and thirst for various things we need or want, or feel we need. Find out about yourself. Examine your attitude toward him.

100

Week after week we have two parts in the Mass. The first part is where we hear the words of Christ and the Old Testament background, and these nourish our spirits, depending on how receptive or how expectant we are. Then you get up and receive him; you take him into your body like food. But it's up to us to make that real. I present my questions to assist you, with your own temperament and background, your experience, and problems you may have with life or your family at the present time. Where do you go for the higher nourishment? And what if you had more of that heart of Jesus? What would that be like?

14

Healing Touch

THEOPHANE BOYD

The Twenty-third Sunday of Ordinary Time

Then he returned from the region of Tyre, and went by way of Sidon towards the Sea of Galilee, in the region of Decapolis. They brought to him a deaf man who had an impediment in his speech; and they begged him to lay his hand upon him. He took him aside in private, away from the crowd, and put his fingers into his ears, and he spat and touched his tongue. Then, looking up to heaven, he sighed and said to him, "Ephphatha," that is, "Be opened." And immediately his ears were opened, his tongue was released, and he spoke plainly. Then Jesus ordered them to tell no one, but the more he ordered them, the more zealously they proclaimed it. They were astounded beyond measure, saying, "He has done everything well; he even makes the deaf to hear and the mute to speak." (Mark 7:31–37)

This is a healing story. Healing stories show up in many religions. They appear in Islam, Hinduism, Buddhism, and certainly in all the shamanic traditions—on every continent of the world.

Here St. Mark is talking about Our Lord healing a deaf person. We used to have a woman here who was quite deaf. She would come into the sacristy before the Mass and present the priest with a microphone. It was an FM radio system, so she had a receiver, and she could hear the prayer and the readings and the sermon. She hasn't been here for several years now, but I met her a year ago and she told me her condition was getting worse: "Now when I go to church I can't hear anything: I can't hear the prayers, I can't hear the readings, I can't hear the sermon, I can't hear the singing." Just imagine that—it's a pretty austere way to live. Just imagine the life outside the church, when all the conversation is going on. She can read lips, but you have to speak slowly and distinctly. It's a pain, and most people won't do it—so she's really isolated in her deafness.

I don't care to address deafness literally, because I don't have experience of it or of dealing frequently with deaf people. I think St. Mark intended that we take the healing symbolically. In the other religions it's the same way. It's intended to be symbolic, not simply a literal hearing impediment such as you might get in a hospital.

Let me suggest a couple of examples. One would be Mother Teresa. In Calcutta, India, where she lived, she would walk through the streets and see people lying on the sidewalks. She listened to them and heard their sickness and aloneness. She would come with a couple of helpers and a van and would pick these people up and bring them to her hospice. She and her fellow sisters never asked them, "Are you Catholic? What insurance do you carry?" She spent her life doing that, and the whole world admired it. She was hearing something other people didn't hear, and she was also speaking a word to them. She was also a great fundraiser; it was as if Christ had touched her ears more deeply with the pain and aloneness of others, and touched her tongue to speak even though she was a frail little woman.

She came to our monastery back in Massachusetts one time. She was getting an honorary doctorate from Holy Cross College, which is about thirty minutes away from our monastery, and one of the monks heard about it and wrote to her, inviting her over. She arrived at the monastery unannounced, after lunch, and I met her. There was nobody to talk to her—after lunch some of the monks take a nap; others go out to work—so I ran to round some up. She came over to the guest house, and sat in the sitting room, and when I finally got back from rounding up people, there was no more room for me, so I sat on the floor in the doorway. I arrived just in time to hear one of the monks asking her, "What can we monks do?"

"Oh," she said, "you have this vocation. You be faithful to what you are doing here. That will be your contribution."

My second example would be Hitler's Holocaust. Who was listening to the cries of those six million Jews? Whose tongue was loosed to speak up? There has been controversy in recent years about Pope Pius XII and how he knew what was going on and didn't speak up. But there were all sorts of people besides the Pope—Germany is a Christian country, and Austria is a Catholic country—and who spoke up? Who heard the cry of those people? Everybody had an excuse, such as "If I speak up, they'll cart me off too, and who's going to take care of my children?" Or "If the bishop spoke up, they'd cart him off and then who would preach the Gospel?" Everybody had an excuse. But it's a scandal, a black spot in the history of Christianity. The question is of hearing, hearing the cry of those people, and speaking out.

This is my way of stretching this notion of deafness, and hearing and speaking. I like to see the story of Jesus curing the deaf man in transcendental terms, suitable for every situation and every age. The story is not about then; it's about now. It's not about him; it's about me. My question, therefore, is: How is *your* hearing? Put up against the hearing of Mother Teresa and the people in Hitler's Germany, how is *your* hearing? What do you *hear*? And what do you *say*? What do you have to say to people?

I think it's a good question for anybody. We can blame a lot of people, but then we come back to ourselves: How can we get that hearing improved? It seems to me that every single person is saying something to me; they've got a claim on me, and do I hear them? We all complain. Young people complain, "My mother doesn't listen to me." The mother complains, "My husband doesn't listen to me." The father complains, "The priest doesn't listen to us." Let's turn back, at least today, on our own hearing. Who am I hearing? How deeply? What am I saying? What's my contribution?

A while back one of the pastors here asked me to come and help out for one weekend at his masses because he wanted to have a healing service. I didn't understand why he needed an extra person to help out, but when I got there I found out, because in his sermon he said to the people, "Usually we have the anointing of the sacrament for people who are physically ill, but besides those physical ills there are other serious maladies. For instance, depression; the inability to forgive somebody; a ferocious temper; an addiction." He invited people to turn around to see what malady they might have, and to come up at offertory time to be anointed by him or me. It was a big church, but it seems to me that everybody in that church came up to be healed, anointed, and to receive the blessing, the touch of Christ.

Today we all face these questions: How is my hearing? How is my tongue? When we come up to receive Our Lord's communion, that's his healing touch. We express that to him, and maybe we go out and do better, feel better, and speak better—as Christ did, and as Mother Teresa did.

Higher Knowledge

THEOPHANE BOYD

The Thirtieth Sunday of Ordinary Time

When the Pharisees learned that Jesus had silenced the Sadducees, they got together, and to disconcert him, one of them put a question, "Master, which is the greatest commandment of the law?" And Jesus said, "You must love the Lord your God with all your heart, with all your soul, and with all your mind. This is the greatest and the first commandment. The second resembles it: 'You must love your neighbor as yourself.' On these two commandments hang the whole law, and the prophets also." (Matthew 22:34–40)

This passage is so familiar that we fall asleep on it. It would take a while to examine the context of the text and how it would have sounded to the people of Our Lord's own time and culture, but let me slip away a little bit and examine the power of the question and the answer from a distance.

Suppose your daughter comes up to you and says, "What's the most important thing in life?" It's not like a kid in school asking a teacher what the most important thing in life is; it's your own daughter, and so all your parenthood and responsibility is challenged. How do you answer? The question sets up a tension, challenges you to sum it all up. And there's another tension between comparing your own answer with the answer of Christ. I think that's quite a valuable thing to do. With tension you get movement; we grow when there's some tension. How would you answer?

I'd like to step back to another image we had several weeks ago where Our Lord was teaching the people at great length, the crowd turned out, and finally one of the apostles leaned over and suggested that his sermon was getting a bit long. Why didn't he send them away, since they hadn't had anything to eat? They could go back into the villages and find something to eat. Our Lord said, "Why don't you feed them?" He was asking something of the apostles. They were leaning on him to do something. Instead, he turned around and said, "Why don't you do something?" One of the disciples says, "I've got a kid here with five loaves and two fishes, is this supposed to feed this crowd?" And Jesus says, "Bring the loaves and fishes over here." So he looks up to God the Father, and gives thanks and distributes the five loaves and two fishes. Then, when the enthusiasm has started to develop—everyone has become aware of what is going on—he dismisses them all, sends the apostles out in their boat, and goes up the mountain alone, staying there several hours praying.

In this little story, you can separate the two answers of Our Lord. He was going up to pray to the Father, and that's what made him run; his energy came from his relationship with the Father: "I and the Father are One. As the Father has sent me, I also send you. As the Father loves me, I love you. I teach the things the Father told me to teach, I do the things the Father [told me to do]." Christ was always coming from the Father.

Christ says the first commandment is to love God with your whole heart, soul, and mind. The second is to love your neighbor as yourself. Christ *lived* it. He *was* it. He's up the mountain for hours; he's not looking at his watch. He's with the Father in utterly sincere prayer. It is worth letting our imagination work on this one. Imagine how Christ's mind was when he was up there alone—nobody around, nobody listening in—and what was going on in his head in relation to the Father. Think about his sincere prayer, and the fact that he was there for hours.

Our Lord didn't stay there for good. He came down, early in the morning. The apostles were on the lake, and the waves were high. He came down, and to get to them he had to walk over the water. He climbed into the boat, and in doing so expressed the sentiment "Love your neighbor as yourself." Jesus didn't stay up there with God. He came down to be with the guys, the boys, his team. When he got in that boat, he was really present with them. That was his group, his family. But notice the continuity: When he came down he brought something down with him, something that stepped into the boat with him. The boat was richer, and the team was richer, for his having been on the mountain. That power and energy that he got from his relationship with the Father was expressed by Christ's coming down to his disciples and getting into the boat.

Not only that, but Our Lord wouldn't allow the disciples to stay in that boat. They stayed for a while, but they were apostles, and he was going to send them out because there were other people in the world who needed to hear his message. They picked up his spirit, which he picked up from the Father. If you apply that spirit in your own life, you might get some interesting light.

The monastic rule is about going up the mountain and being face to face with God. The monastic community is like a small boat, with all its limitations and shortcomings. Yet which is better, to be up on the mountain alone or be with the group? Then there's not just the boat, the monastery; there are other people in the world. What is your boat? What is your little team? Is it your family, your profession, your parish, your town? How do you think about the responsibility for that group you live with? Is there some "going up the mountain" for you? How would you go up? Do you go up somewhere for some higher wisdom, for courage, for joy? We all have our wisdom, our experience, our knowledge—and it's valuable. We are smarter today than we were ten years ago—but the question is worth thinking about: Is there some space where you can go up and learn some more, become wiser, more loving?

If so, where would you go? Some people go to a monastery, some to the Bible, some to Mecca, some to the library, some to a bank. Where do you go for higher wisdom, so that when you come back to your team, your group, your family, whatever it is, you have something higher and better to offer. How much priority does that have for you? Is it important or not? Is it worth a lot of time? Do you feel guilty for not making time for it?

Some people tend to stay down in the boat. They don't go up. Some people want to stay up on the mountain and don't want to come down with the guys. Do you notice anybody outside your little boat? One of the problems of religion is we get in our little boats and then from our boats we judge everybody else. It's been going on for centuries with all the different religions.

Christ stands for something different. He stays on the mountain a good while and then comes down. He does both, and that's a lesson for us. He won't allow his apostles to think that the whole point is that they be huddled safely together. "That's not what I brought down from the Father," Jesus might have said.

This is the challenge for all of us. When your daughter asks that question, "What's the most important thing?" think about how you would answer, and put your answer up against these answers. See what tension arises, and what it does to you. There's a trick in reading a sacred text. Don't turn the page. Stay there till you blush, or laugh, or cry, or are moved. Maybe just stay there until you are moved from where you are to some higher place, never mind what the priest said in the sermon. It can linger throughout the day.

16

The Publican, the Pharisee, and Me

WILLIAM MENINGER

The Thirtieth Sunday of Ordinary Time

He also told this parable to some who trusted in themselves that they were righteous and regarded others with contempt: "Two men went up to the Temple to pray, one a Pharisee and the other a tax collector. The Pharisee, standing by himself, was praying thus: 'God, I thank you that I am not like other people: thieves, rogues, adulterers, or even like this tax collector. I fast twice a week; I give a tenth of all my income.' But the tax collector, standing far off, would not even look up to heaven, but was beating his breast and saying, 'God, be merciful to me, a sinner!' I tell you, this man went down to his home justified rather than the other; for all who exalt themselves will be humbled, but all who humble themselves will be exalted." (Luke 18:9–14)

Today's gospel has only six verses, but it is an absolute gem. It is framed by an introductory comment, given to us by St. Luke, and a conclusion that sums up the meaning and purpose of the parable. In the introduction Luke says that Jesus "told this parable to some who trusted in themselves that they were righteous and regarded others with contempt." In the conclusion he sums it up in this way: "All who exalt themselves will be humbled, but all who humble themselves will be exalted."

There are four people involved in this story. Jesus is the storyteller. Then there are the characters of the story, the Pharisee and the publican (tax collector). The fourth person we shall identify in a moment.

From the New Testament and from other sources we know a great deal about the Pharisees. The word *Pharisees* means "the separated ones." They were separated in the sense that, unlike many of the Jews, they observed very strictly a large body of regulations taken from the Hebrew scriptures and also from an oral tradition added on to the scriptures to interpret these regulations. They were the canon lawyers of the Jews, accepted as experts in legal interpretations. These interpretations of Jewish law were considered to be expressions of the will of God for his people and were taken, at least by the Pharisees, very seriously. This was not easy to do, as some of these laws were very complicated and even required financial resources that the common Jew did not have. These common Jews, the non-observers, were looked down upon by many of the Pharisees. They considered them to be sinners, not because they actually lived immoral lives but because they did not observe the laws that the Pharisees claimed governed morality.

In Jesus' time in Palestine, there were about 6,000 Pharisees. After the destruction of Jerusalem in 70 A.D., the Pharisees were responsible for the survival of Judaism as a religion. Their opponents, the priests or Sadducees, were killed in the destruction of the Temple or fled to Damascus, where many became Christians.

In the gospels we often see the party of the Pharisees opposing Jesus both openly and, through various plottings, secretly. It is interesting to note that if we were to put Jesus into a category, he would best fit in with the Pharisees. St. Paul certainly was one. As he said to the gathering of Jewish priests in Jerusalem, "I am a Pharisee and the son of Pharisees" (Acts 23:6). Later he said, "As for observance of the law, I was a Pharisee" (Philippians 3:5). It was precisely as a Pharisee that Paul persecuted the followers of Jesus.

The tax collector, or publican, belonged to a class of people despised by the rest of the Jews. The publicans collected the taxes for the despised Roman conquerors of Palestine and were considered as hirelings and no better than traitors. They made a substantial living by what they could skim, legally or otherwise, from the taxes they collected. The phrase "publicans and sinners" was often found in the mouths of the Pharisees. There is no record of such people being opposed to Jesus, whose attitude toward them was one of friendly admonition and forgiveness, even on occasion dining in their homes. St. Matthew, the apostle, was a tax collector. Indeed, he was at his table collecting the customs when he first encountered Jesus in Jericho.

This leads us to the fourth person in this story, without whom it would be meaningless: the listener, the one for whom the story is told, you and me. We are embraced and summoned into the story and we must hear the opening statement of Luke as referring to ourselves. "He also told this parable to some who trusted in themselves that they were righteous and regarded others with contempt."

The Pharisee was not necessarily wrong in acknowledging his good points. "I fast twice a week; I give a tenth of all my income." But his meaning was that he was righteous, that is, acceptable to God, because of his religious observances, which he defined by contrasting them with the defects of others. The tax collector, Jesus tells us, went home justified, not because of his observances, but because he acknowledged his unworthiness before God.

The great sin of the Pharisee was certainly not in his observances of the written and unwritten laws. By and large, Jesus also observed them. Rather it was by defining his goodness in contrast to the defects of others, and by having such a low opinion of God as to think that God was mollified by his petty deeds.

This story is a call for humility. We are called to acknowledge the truth about ourselves. Are the things that we say and do really of such import that we can lay them before God and expect them somehow to benignly influence the infinite deity to extend us his favor? Humility is the foundation of all the virtues. Unless we truly know where we stand and where we begin our journey toward God, we can never get there. As Jesus says, we are to do all that is required of us and then simply acknowledge ourselves as unprofitable servants. Otherwise, as the Pharisee did, we build our houses on sand.

If we make our own prayer the prayer of the publican, "God be merciful to me, a sinner," we do not put our trust in ourselves and in our own deeds. Rather we turn to Jesus as the one in whom we live and move and have our being. God then does not see us as the sinners that we are, covered by the scars and stains of our past sins. Rather he looks at us and sees his beloved son in whom he is well pleased. It is in this way that we go home justified. "All who exalt themselves will be humbled, but all who humble themselves will be exalted."

17

Authority as Service

Thomas Keating

The Thirty-First Sunday of Ordinary Time

Addressing the people and his disciples, Jesus said.
"The Scribes and Pharisees occupy the chair of
Moses. You must therefore do what they tell you
and listen to what they say. But do not be guided
by what they do, since they do not practice what
they preach. They tie up heavy burdens and lay
them on people's shoulders, but will they lift a finger to move them? Not they. Everything they do is
to attract attention, like wearing broader headbands
and longer tassels, like wanting to take the place of
honor at banquets, and the front seats in the synagogues, being greeted obsequiously in the market
squares, and having people call them Rabbi.

"You, however, must not allow yourselves to be
called Rabbi, since you have only one Master and
you are all brothers and sisters. You must call no one

on earth your father, since you have only one Father, and he is in heaven. Nor must you allow yourselves to be called teachers, because you have only one Teacher, the Christ. The greatest among you must be your servant. Those who exalt themselves will be humbled, and those who humble themselves will be exalted. (Matthew 23:2–12)

The gospel this morning is about how to exercise authority, or rather, how not exercise it. The last line summarizes Jesus' advice: "Those who exalt themselves will be humbled, and those who humble themselves will be exalted."

Humility is the acceptance of all reality: God, ourselves, everybody else, everything that is or happens. The spirit that Jesus insinuates into the whole exercise of authority and how we experience it—both in exercising it and receiving it—is significant for all human affairs, and not just for the Church. Assertiveness of any kind will not get us anywhere, because it always stimulates resistance, and resistance elicits an emotional response that makes it difficult to talk about the real issues. Once issues are tinged by emotions, hidden agendas arise.

In this situation, discernment regarding what needs to be done becomes more and more obscure. Someone has to come along who can cut through that nonsense and bring us to a humble state of mind. This begins with the acceptance of reality. It is reality that needs to be addressed, not our feelings about it.

Of course, our feelings are very helpful and accurate at times. They are clues as to what is happening both inside us and in the situation, but they are not the deciding factors. For, while our emotions are valuable, it is what we do with them that is most important, We *are not* our emotions. We are a concentration of a number of delicate and interrelated faculties, In fact, the human organism is a mass of relationships which have to be put in proper order for the organism to be at peace. And it is humility that orders them. From the space of humility we are able to address with honesty and clarity our own problems and those of other people.

There are many examples in the gospels provided by the disciples and friends of Jesus about what *not* to do. One example concerns the sons of Zebedee (Mark 3:17). These brothers were nicknamed "sons of thunder," so they must have been fairly formidable characters. The two sons asked their mother to ask Jesus—a delicate way of approaching a situation that was hard for them to face head-on (Matthew 20:21)—to sit at the right and left hand of Jesus in his kingdom (Mark 13:36). Jesus did not rebuke them. Instead, he told them they didn't know for what they were asking. In effect, he was saying, "Can you fulfill the requirements for that position? What is your resume?" Their resume was not too good. They had wanted to call down fire from heaven on the inhospitable Samaritans who had treated them poorly. They were not likely candidates for the right and left hand of the God of love.

Jesus' question implied, "Why do you want to be on the right and left hand of the Messiah? Why do you want to be in authority? What is your *motive* for wanting to control other people?" Here, it is not the situation that is the problem. It is the drive for happiness that believes firmly that it has to control persons, events, and even God—if we could get away with it.

We can't get away with it, because God loves us too much. As the contemplative life deepens and the spiritual journey frees us from our preconceived ideas and prepackaged values, we are empowered to experience our emotions just as they are and then to decide what to do with them. Sometimes it is appropriate to be angry and manifest anger. It takes a very well-balanced person to succeed in manifesting anger appropriately.

Jesus must have been in a towering rage when he threw the moneychangers out of the temple (John 2:14–16). The latter must have been scared to death. The look on Jesus' face must have been terrifying as he turned over their tables and shouted, "Get out of here!" We don't know what epithets he used to reinforce his position, but the moneychangers got out of there as fast as they could.

Just anger is irresistible. I was once a guest in a Catholic summer camp whose director was great man. Some former counselors had come back for a holiday weekend and were staying at the guesthouse. One night, they were keeping everybody including the young campers awake, drinking plenty of liquor and partying hard. The noise was deafening.

All of a sudden the director appeared at the door and said just two words, "Get out!" The men and women took one look at his face and fled through the doors and windows. They could not get away from that face fast enough.

The purpose of being angry or exercising authority is to respond to the present moment appropriately. What needs to be remembered is that after we have expressed the emotion, it ends, and we move on to the next event. But when anger lingers in our awareness we build destructive kinds of responses—such as long-term grudges, an unwillingness to forgive, inflexibility, or defensiveness.

We can overreact to our feelings; everyone does that. If we apologize, hopefully the situation is over. But when we over-identify with anger or other emotions, they become a part of us. We begin to think we *are* angry when we only have angry feelings. With God's help and the use of our reason and will we can decide not to act out. Acting out reinforces the dynamics of the false self and the unconscious drives for happiness that are directed to symbols in the culture that we mistakenly identify as happiness.

Therefore, in exercising authority, whether as a parent or a leader in a community, this gospel tells us what *not* to do. We are not to make a point of our status, superior position, or power. Real power—and this is the heart of the Gospel—does not come from asserting authority. It comes from the power of love. Love is the only irresistible force in the universe; everything else produces a reaction. And while love does not always seem to win, selfless love that perseveres *always* wins.

This is the mystery that Jesus is trying to communicate to us: the greatest gift of the Gospel is not in the power of exercising authority but the power to go on loving no matter what happens. This is sometimes called servant leadership. This is service in the sense of *self-sacrifice*, of experiencing the needs of others as one's own. The power of authority is manifested when it has to confront or correct somebody, when it does so not out of exasperation or attachment to some list of rules, but from a real concern for the person's welfare. This may mean that you are willing to sacrifice your own peace of mind and risk, perhaps, their anger and loss of friendship in order to tell them what you feel about their conduct that might be harmful or wrong.

Let us not betray the great gifts that God has given us as disciples of the Gospel by exercising authority out of revenge, self-interest, or status. Let us instead exercise authority out of love in order to manifest God. If we correct not out of anger but always out of love, then the people we are trying to help will have the greatest possibility of change. Whenever selfish motivation is present in the correction or in the exercise of authority, the same thing happens as at the time of the Reformation. It is rejected. True greatness is the ability to serve. That is the root meaning of the word "authority": the capacity to lead not by the exercise of power but by love.

People of the Kingdom

JOSEPH BOYLE

The Sunday of Christ the King

Jesus said to his disciples, "When the Son of Man comes in his glory, escorted by all the angels, then will he take his seat on his throne of glory. All the nations will be assembled before him, and he will separate people one from another as a shepherd separates sheep from goats. He will place the sheep on his right hand and the goats on his left. Then the King will say to those on his right hand: 'Come, you whom my Father has blessed, take for your heritage the kingdom prepared for you since the foundation of the world. For I was hungry and you gave me food, I was thirsty and you gave me drink, I was a stranger and you made me welcome, naked and you clothed me, sick and you visited me, in prison and you came to see me.' Then the virtuous will say to him in reply: 'Lord when did we see you hungry and feed you, or thirsty and give you drink? When did we see you a stranger and make you welcome, naked and clothe you, sick or in prison and go to see you?' And the King will answer: 'I tell you solemnly, insofar as you did this to one of the least of these brothers or sisters of mine, you did it to me.'

"Next he will say to those on his left hand: 'Go away from me, with your curse upon you, to the eternal fire prepared for the Devil and his angels. For I was hungry and you never gave me food, I was thirsty and you never gave me anything to drink, I was a stranger and you never made me welcome, naked and you never clothed me, sick and in prison and you never visited me.' Then it will be their turn to ask: 'Lord, when did we see you hungry or thirsty, a stranger or naked, sick or in prison, and did not come to your help?' Then he will answer: 'I tell you solemnly, insofar as you neglected to do this to one of the least of these, you neglected to do it to me.' And they will go away to eternal punishment, and the virtuous to eternal life."
(Matthew 25:31–46)

The Sunday of Christ the King is the last Sunday of the Church year. The following Sunday is Advent and the beginning of a whole new cycle centered around the birth of Christ. However, this Sunday acts as a way to wind up the old year. What the Church has done on this last Sunday of the year is to make it a feast, the solemnity of Christ the

King. This is a relatively modern development. Indeed, it was only in the last century that the feast of Christ the King was inaugurated. Those of us old enough to remember can recall when this feast used to be the last Sunday in October. Then, with the reforms in the liturgy established by the Second Vatican Council in the 1960s, it got moved to the very last Sunday of the Church year. So here we are.

Some of you might like that title, Christ the King. There are parishes and schools and so on with that title. Others are not so helped by it. The word "king" does not carry some of the connotations for us as it did a few generations back or in other cultures. But that doesn't really matter for understanding this feast, because the feast is talking about Christ as our Lord, Christ our leader, the one whom we are following. Christ is the one we put our faith in and have given our lives to, and who, in fact, has given life to us.

This is the focus of this particular Sunday, and, in making this the feast for the last Sunday of the year, the Church gives us a chance to encapsulate in a brief and focused way the message of Christ—what he is about. It also allows us to reflect on that message and see how much we have absorbed it and how much it has given shape to who we are.

This is what I would like to explore with you. First of all, we should put aside whatever exalted connotations we get from the title Christ the King—anything that might smack of luxury, or easy living, or extravagance that we associate in our imaginations with kingship, such as power, privilege, and so on. All of these associations are shredded by texts we get from the scripture.

I am thinking, for instance, of James and John when they were following Christ, before they had really gotten his message and had just had the illumination of being in the presence of the Messiah. They asked their mother to ask Jesus if they could be the ones sitting on Christ's right and left in the kingdom. They didn't know what the kingdom was about. Jesus told them, "Those seats my Father gives away, but can you drink the cup I am going to drink; can you really follow my path?" James and John said they could, not knowing what it would entail. In the end they did drink the cup.

Jesus continued, "I came not to be served, but to serve, and to give my life as a ransom for many." This is what his kingdom and his lordship are about. They are about the love in the heart of Christ that enabled him to pour himself out, for us, as our ransom, that we might have life. Since the Sunday readings are on a three-year cycle, on this feast day next year, the gospel reading will be the dialogue between Pilate and Jesus—Jesus, broken, stripped down, beaten, and yet talking about the kingdom with Pilate. Pilate and Jesus are talking about two different kingdoms. The year after next on this day, we will see Jesus on the cross, with the sign placed by Pilate over his head proclaiming him "Jesus of Nazareth, King of the Jews."

This is what we mean when we talk about "king." It is a king who loved his people so much that he gave his life completely, a shepherd who laid down his life for his sheep.

In the gospel passage that begins the chapter, we see Christ as the king in judgment, and the emphasis then shifts to us, the people of the kingdom. In this particular kingdom there is only one norm of citizenship, only one thing that counts: Do we have in us the same kind of love that our Lord has, our Lord who laid down his life? Do we have the same kind of love, a love that goes out to other people, that can pour itself out in caring, that can reach out to the needy, thirsty, hungry, imprisoned, sick, and so on, whatever those needs are? Do we have in us the same kind of life that Christ the Lord has? If we do, then we are invited into the kingdom—in fact, we are already in the kingdom. If we do not, then there is no relationship, even if we say "Lord, Lord." Simply put, the relationship of deep inner life isn't there.

When we talk about service in our day and age—taking care of others and watching out for their needs—we have to recognize that we sometimes act charitably for all the wrong reasons. A lot of the things that look like serving and caring for people are in fact extensions of our insecurity, our need to please people, our desire for acceptance or avoiding conflict, and other such codependent behaviors. There are many books to help us work through our processes and growth and development, but I want to emphasize that acting from these reasons is *not* what I mean when I explore Christ and the kingdom and loving service.

What needs to motivate us is the motivation we see in Christ. Christ is somebody who always walked upright and functioned from a deep inner freedom. He did what he did because he *chose* to do it, because he loved in a way that offered service in a mature, free manner. In addition, Jesus' service reached out in ever-widening circles. He went wherever there was need. He broke all of the boundaries that were common in his time, his culture, and among his people. He was always going outside, spreading the good news. This is what we need to do, too. It is easy to be kind to people who are kind to us; such interactions are pleasant and allow society to run quite smoothly. But, as Jesus says in another place in the gospel, "For if you love those who love you, what reward will you get? Do not even the gentiles do as much?" (Matthew 5:46)

Again, such love is not bad, and it makes our lives pleasant. But only when we push past these comfort circles and really open up can we understand Jesus' notion of service. This doesn't mean that we don't also have to be forgiving and reconciling and of service within our close relationships. What it means is that Jesus doesn't let us stay there. He pushes us outward, in the same way that God reaches out to us. Just as God's love pours itself into creation, so we have a world that came out of God's love. And God poured himself into redemption in giving us his son. It is this kind of outgoing love that is the heart of God, and which we see as the heart of Christ. It is this kind of thing we look for when we contemplate the meaning of the kingdom.

All of us are searching for it in different ways. We are all different, with different gifts, talents, situations in life, contacts, and places where we are. The kingdom takes a different shape with each one of us, but we all have the same energy of the Christ within us and pushing us outward.

The Burden of Service

To many reading this, the service I have described may seem fairly burdensome, almost unnatural, pushing against the grain. To some extent, when we change our habits and begin to move out of ego into service for others we do need a push. However, the people who have really worked at practicing Jesus' type of service have written that such service is not unnatural. As a matter of fact, the service fits with who we are and becomes a deep happiness in us.

A person who followed Jesus' service was Albert Schweitzer (1875–1965), who was, among his many other achievements, both a scholar of scripture and a medical doctor. In middle age, Schweitzer left Europe and went to Africa to serve as a medical doctor, where he remained for decades. When he was there Schweitzer said, "The only ones among you who will be really happy are those who have sought and found how to serve." What this tells me is that, when we push beyond our boundaries so that we get to experience in ourselves the person that God really made, we will find contentment as well.

It seems to me that we have some help along the way of service. The first assistance is Jesus' teaching, such as the Sermon on the Mount, his instructions, and stories such as the Good Samaritan, the man who stops to help the injured person. All these help us let Jesus fill in a little bit what is expected of us.

More than these, however, on a deeper level it is Jesus himself who models service for us. Jesus didn't just talk about service. I am sure there are many of us who have run into teachers who can talk about things, but when we look at their lives we scratch our heads and wonder whether these teachers really believe what they are saying. However, when we see Christ, we see something real and attractive, and we can take into our prayer his example.

Beyond this level, however, there is yet another level of assistance, and this is the fact that Christ is not only a teacher and a model, he is the Lord, and is able to share life with us, from the inside. Just as he teaches us the meaning of service by modeling it, so he reaches us from the inside by being in union with each one of us. We take quiet time and quiet prayer in order to contact Christ and God at that deep level of our being, so that out of that union, these actions and behaviors can manifest. This is why we come to Eucharist, and make contact with the sharing of life that is in this bread and wine. Christ really shares his life for us and becomes an inner resource for us so that, in doing the things he talks about, we have an energy from within that can help move us to do it.

The scriptures speak about this experience in different ways. They speak of the Lord who breathed his spirit into us, so that we can say we have Christ's spirit within us. Once more, however, we have to cooperate, to open ourselves up and stretch ourselves, take risks. But it is not only us that's pushing outward. It is Christ the Lord within us who is doing it. Another image, a particular favorite of mine, is the one that Jesus uses in his farewell discourse before he died, "I am the vine, and you are the branches." What Jesus means is that the life that is within him as the vine is the same life that flows into us, the branches, where the life bears fruit.

This is what I believe we mean when we celebrate this feast day of Christ the King. We both celebrate Christ as the one who has completed his work, died, risen, and ascended, and honor the Christ who is still working within each one of us, bringing forth the same kind of loving service and actions and behavior he modeled. In this way, we have a role to play in this feast, because a king is nothing without his subjects, the people of his kingdom. What, we might ask, is a vine without branches and fruit?

I was in California once for a workshop, and we were visiting one of our brethren in Napa Valley, a great wine-producing area. However, because it was February, when we looked at the great vineyards, all we could see were little chunks of pruned-down vine protected from the cold. But we knew that, come the summer, with heat and water, the vine would sprout into branches and the branches into fruit, and from that fruit we would get wine. A whole new world would occur.

For me, the growth of the grape is a little bit like the relationship between us and Christ the king. As Christ pours his energy, his life-giving sap, his grace and spirit, into us, then that vine is filled and extended in the fruit of the branches. One such branch of the vine was Mother Teresa. She was such a major figure in our world. Yet, when you saw her and her sisters with her and the work they did for the dying in Calcutta, it was possible to see the lordship of Christ present, people of the kingdom alive with his life.

The kingdom is alive in Catholic Worker soup kitchens and in those individual deeds in which people stretch and you can begin to see the love of Christ revealed in them, the Spirit active and working. This is why the feast of Christ the King is a feast—there is something to celebrate. It is a time to reflect on the presence of the Lord Christ in our life; to examine to what extent his life, his values, and his spirit shapes our deeds. On this day, we can ask ourselves whether anybody looking at us would guess that Christ is our Lord. We can ask ourselves whether we allow his life to be the life that pulses in us.